WORDLESS BOOKS

SO MUCH TO SAY!

GILDA MARTINEZ-ALBA AND
JUDITH CRUZADO-GUERRERO, EDITORS

 tesol press

Design and layout by Capitol Communications, LLC, Crofton, Maryland, USA
Printed by Gasch Printing, LLC, Odenton, Maryland, USA

TESOL Press
TESOL International Association
1925 Ballenger Avenue
Alexandria, Virginia, 22314 USA
www.tesol.org

Senior Manager, Publications: Myrna Jacobs
Cover Design: Citrine Sky Design
Copyeditor: Elizabeth Pontiff
Reviewers: Michelle Marchiano and Timothy Hartigan

TESOL Book Publications Committee:
    Robyn L. Brinks Lockwood, Chair
    Elizabeth Byleen
    Margo DelliCarpini
    Robert Freeman
    Deoksoon Kim
    Ilka Kostka
    Guofang Li
    John Liontas, Past Chair
    Gilda Martinez-Alba
    Allison Rainville
    Jason Stegemoller
    Adrian J. Wurr

ISBN 9781942223337
Library of Congress Control Number 2015944180

CONTENTS

Each of the following wordless or almost wordless books has one lesson created by a teacher for a teacher or parent. The books are grouped based first on the pictures and then on the English proficiency levels needed for the lesson. The following key will help you find a lesson that works to develop speaking, listening, reading, or writing. Most lessons focus on speaking, listening, and writing because the books are wordless.

*SL = Speaking and listening objectives

*R = Reading objectives

*W = Writing objectives

INTRODUCTION

by Gilda Martinez-Alba and Judith Cruzado-Guerrero

> *The relatively recent appearance of wordless books is an antecedent of an ancient form of communication which our ancestors used to recount hunts, daily events, military incursions, and even Bible stories by using various media, including caves, tapestry, and stained-glass windows. (Dowhower, 1997, p. 58)*

In 1932 the first wordless book for children in the United States was published: *What Whiskers Did* (Caroll, 1932). Not many were published for several years after that. However, in the 1960s, 44 wordless books were published in the United States; in the 1970s, 317 were published; and in the 1980s, 408 were published. (Dowhower, 1997). Why did wordless books become so popular? Because they are very appealing, and teachers have found many benefits to using them with young children, adolescents, adults, and English learners.

Wordless books can be very engaging when used with English learners of all levels and ages to build English skills. Students can feel successful, regardless of their literacy level in any language. Wordless books can be used to develop oral language, vocabulary, listening, comprehension, writing skills, and much more. What makes them so beneficial is that they are full of visuals, which English learners need to help them with comprehension (Peregoy & Boyle, 2013). Moreover, there are no wrong answers when making up a story about a wordless book, which provides a nonthreatening environment for language learning.

With wordless books, K–12 and adult students can be authors and write the story that they interpret from the pictures. This can lead to a rich discussion about students' thoughts based on the illustrations. A study at the University of Utah showed that wordless picture books can lead to richer discussions than picture books with text (Lindauer, 1988). Since then, numerous studies have shown the benefits of using wordless picture books:

- Students learn how to make meaning from illustrations (Arizpe, 2013);
- Close reading of illustrations helps develop discussions (Ramos & Ramos, 2011);
- Students can work on comprehension, such as making inferences (Stahl, 2014);
- Students improve their writing (McAdam & Sinkie, 2013);
- Wordless books support biliteracy development (Jung & Commeyras, 2012);
- Students' motivation is improved (Arizpe, 2013); and
- Parents can use wordless books to interact with their children to develop reading motivation (Le Roux & Costandius, 2013).

Because one of the main goals of reading is comprehension, teachers want their students to understand stories covered in class. Thus, teachers can use wordless books to explain comprehension strategies. Then students can reread the stories to work on their speaking skills by talking through the stories and verbalizing their inferences. Students can even develop bilingual skills if their teachers provide them with time to work on using two languages.

Parents wanting to participate in their child's education can read the story to their child in any language, even if they cannot read or write in any language. This can potentially lead to students becoming interested in books, while showing parents how they can help with their child's academic progress. To make home connections, teachers can provide students with lessons from the book, and then have students go home and re-create or share the activities with their parents.

When reviewing wordless books, specific titles lend themselves to different types of instruction. For example, *Flotsam* (Wiesner, 1991) is a complicated story about a camera's travels in the ocean that has a wealth of vocabulary that can be discussed. In this book, *Flotsam* has a lesson for speaking and listening in which students are encouraged to talk about the illustrations and later about a mystery bag's contents related to the story.

On the other hand, *Chalk* (Thomson, 2010) is a simpler yet exciting book about drawings that come to life, which can be used to discuss story structure. The lesson in this book for *Chalk* emphasizes writing and speaking, and students write a script and make a movie based on the book.

This book will take readers on a journey through 23 wordless or almost wordless books. Teachers created engaging lesson ideas, each one connected to a highly rated wordless book, so you do not have to research which wordless books are worth your while. The lesson ideas are aligned with the Common Core State Standards for English Language Arts (National Governors Association Center for Best Practices and Council of Chief State School Officers, 2010; copyright © 2010 National Governors Association Center for Best Practices and Council of Chief State School Officers. All rights reserved.), specifically in reading, writing, speaking and listening and include a range of grade levels on the rubrics to provide you with a quick overview of how the standards get more involved as grade level increases. You can look for the grade level you are interested in on the Common Core website and cut and paste the appropriate standards for your students into the editable rubrics provided on the companion website for this book, **www.tesol.org/wordless**. You may find different Common Core State Standards work better for your students' needs than the examples provided, these are simply suggestions provided by the teachers that created the lessons. We have also included TESOL Standards (TESOL International Association, 2006) in the objectives section of the lessons. In addition, a list of vocabulary words is provided for each lesson. Last but not least, interesting related websites and apps are listed for each lesson. We hope you have the opportunity to use many if not all of the ideas in this book, using them as is or tweaking them to make them work for your students.

References

Arizpe, E. (2013). Making-meaning from wordless (or nearly wordless) picture books: What educational research expects and what readers have to say. *Cambridge Journal of Education, 43*(2), 163–176. http://dx.doi.org// 10.1080/0305764X.2013.767879

Caroll, R. (1932). *What whiskers did.* New York, NY: Macmillan.

Dowhower, S. (1997). Wordless books: Promise and possibilities, a genre come of age. *Yearbook of the American Reading Forum.* Retrieved from http://americanreadingforum.org/yearbook/yearbooks/97_yearbook /pdf/06_Dowhower.pdf

Jung, Y. S., & Commeyras, M. (2012). Using wordless picture books to support biliteracy development: The case study of a six-year-old Korean ESL boy. *Primary English Education, 18*(2), 407–427.

Le Roux, A., & Costandius, E. (2013). Wordless picture books in parent-child reading in a South African context. *Acta Academia, 45*(2), 27–58.

Lindauer, S. L. K. (1988). Wordless books: An approach to visual literacy. *Children's Literature in Education, 19*(3), 136–142.

McAdam, J. E., & Sinkie, H. (2013). Picture books: Opening pathways for new arrival children. *English 4–11,* 16–20.

National Governors Association Center for Best Practices and Council of Chief State School Officers. (2010). *Common Core State Standards English Language Arts Standards.* Washington, DC: author.

Peregoy, S., & Boyle, O. (2013). *Reading, writing, and learning in ESL: A Resource Book for Teaching K–12 English Learners.* Boston, MA: Pearson.

Ramos, A. M., & Ramos, R. (2011). Ecoliteracy through imagery: A close reading of two wordless picture books. *Children's Literature in Education, 42,* 325–339. http://dx.doi.org/10.1007/s10583-011-9142-3

Stahl, K. A. D. (2014). Fostering inference generation with emergent and novice readers. *The Reading Teacher, 67*(5), 384–388. http://dx.doi.org/10.1002 /trtr.1230

TESOL International Association. (2006). *Pre-K–12 English Language proficiency standards.* Alexandria, VA: author.

Thomson, B. (2010). *Chalk.* New York, NY: Amazon Children's Publishing.

Wiesner, D. (1991). *Flotsam.* New York, NY: Clarion Books.

STORIES WITH EASY PICTURES TO FOLLOW

SHAPES, SHAPES, SHAPES

by Tana Hoban

Lesson by Lizabeth S. Kurtz

Level	Beginning
Preparation Time	5 minutes
Length of Lesson	Up to 45 minutes
Objective	Students will draw objects from their environment using shapes from the story. Then, in small groups, they will describe the shape and the object they drew.

Materials

- *Shapes, Shapes, Shapes* by Tana Hoban (New York, NY: Greenwillow Books, 1986)
- Shape cutouts
- "Shake Your Shape" song (*Math All around Me* CD by Jack Hartmann available at www.jackhartmann.com/math-all-around-me-cd/)

Vocabulary

- circle
- oval
- rectangle
- rhombus
- square
- triangle

Procedure

1. Engage students in a movement activity by having them shake shapes to incorporate music and movement. Give each student a shape. When the song says the name of the student's shape he or she shakes it in the air (e.g., when song says, "shake your circle," everyone holding a circle shakes it in the air). This helps students recognize shape names and engages them with songs and music.

2. Lead a discussion describing the shapes and their attributes. Give students an opportunity to turn and talk to a partner about where they have seen shapes in their world (e.g., A clock is a circle. A door is a rectangle.). Then, have students share their answers with the group.

3. Chart answers as students list them. Draw a picture and label it with the word to help students learn the vocabulary. This chart will be used as a reference for the next activity.

4. Read the story aloud. On the first page, model describing the shapes seen in the picture (e.g., "I see a triangle as the shape of a sail."). Then call on students to share what shapes they see for the remainder of the book.

5. After "reading" the book and looking for shapes, have class members discuss what shapes they saw in the book and add any new ideas to their chart.

6. Have each student choose one shape (already cut out for them) to turn into a picture. Students can reference the chart for ideas or come up with a new one.

7. Have small groups of students discuss what shapes they picked (to work on shape identification) and what real-life objects they turned their shapes into (to connect them to their life or the book). Place each page into a class book, and put the book in the classroom library.

Assessment

The pictures students created using a shape will show whether students can apply what they learned from the story (i.e., turning a shape into a real picture). Students will also share their ideas in small groups and use their speaking skills to describe their shapes and the pictures they created.

Additional Resources

Additional Shape Read Alouds

- *The Shape of Things* by Dayle Ann Dodds (St. Louis, MO: Turtleback Books, 1996).
- *When a Line Bends . . . A Shape Begins* by Rhonda Gowler Greene (Boston, MA: Houghton Mifflin Harcourt, 2001).
- *The Greedy Triangle* by Marilyn Burns (New York, NY: Scholastic, 2008).

Related Websites

Shape identification quizzes for additional practice with identifying shapes—
- www.ixl.com/math/kindergarten/identify-shapes
- www.ixl.com/math/kindergarten/identify-shapes-ii.

Pattern-block games to practice using shapes to make pictures—
   http://illuminations.nctm.org/Activity.aspx?id=3577.

Related Apps

- PrestoBingo Shapes Lite (free)—find hidden shapes in a picture. Available on iTunes.
- Shape Match (free)—play memory to match shapes. Available on Google play.
- Learn Shapes: Sorting Activity (free)—sort shapes, build shapes, count shapes, match shapes, and make patterns with shapes. Available on Google play.

Further Reading

Busy Teacher. (2014). *How to teach shapes.* Retrieved from http://busyteacher .org/3854-how-to-teach-shapes.html.

TESOL PreK–12 English Language Proficiency Standards

Standard 1: English language learners communicate for social, intercultural, and instructional purposes within the school setting.

Standard 2: English language learners communicate information, ideas, and concepts necessary for academic success in the area of language arts.

Standard 3: English language learners communicate information, ideas, and concepts necessary for academic success in the area of mathematics.

Common Core State Standards ELA Suggested Connections

The following are the Common Core State Standards for English Language Arts that are aligned with this lesson. The rubric on the next page includes a sampling of grade levels to show how the standards get more complex at higher grade levels.

Speaking and Listening: SL.K.2; SL.K.4; SL.K.5; SL.K.6

SHAPES, SHAPES, SHAPES

CCSS Sample Rubric

Go to www.tesol.org/wordless to complete the rubric by adding your grade level standards from the Common Core website.

Speaking and Listening: http://www.corestandards.org/ELA-Literacy/SL /introduction/

	Grading Criteria			
	Outstanding 10	**Adequate 8–9**	**Developing 1–7**	**Not Present 0**
	All of the criteria are present and fully developed.	Most of the criteria are present and adequately developed.	Some of the criteria are present and somewhat developed.	None of the criteria are present.
Standards	**Teacher's Comments**			
SL.K.2. Confirm understanding of a text read aloud or information presented orally or through other media by asking and answering questions about key details. *or*				
SL.K.4. Describe familiar people, places, things, and events, and with prompting and support, provide additional detail. *or*				
SL.K.5. Add drawings or other visual displays to descriptions as described to provide additional detail. *or*				
SL.K.6. Speak audibly and express thoughts, feelings, and ideas clearly.				
Total points				

PANCAKES FOR BREAKFAST

by Tomie DePaola

Lesson by Lizabeth S. Kurtz

Level	Beginning
Preparation Time	5 minutes
Length of Lesson	30 minutes
Objective	Students will use a combination of drawing, dictating, and writing to share their prediction of the story.

Materials

- *Pancakes for Breakfast* by Tomie DePaola (New York, NY: Harcourt, 1978)
- Picture cards (flour, baking powder, butter, sugar, salt, eggs, milk)
- Tablet computer or pictures for developing inferences
- Journals

Vocabulary

- baking powder
- batter
- butter
- cooking
- eggs
- flour
- milk
- mixing
- pancakes
- salt
- sugar

Procedure

1. Review vocabulary picture cards of the ingredients to make pancakes and have a discussion about whether students have ever baked something. Have students turn and talk to a partner to allow them to share with one peer before sharing to the class.

2. As a warm-up, have students look at pictures on a tablet computer (or on printed copies) to practice looking for information (clues) and using prior knowledge to make inferences. Explain that when books have no words, students have to use information (clues) and what they already know (prior knowledge) to make inferences (guesses) about what is happening in the story.

3. For the first page, model how to make inferences and make up the words in the story. Think aloud: "I see there is snow on the ground, so I will make a guess that it is winter. There is a little house or cottage. I wonder who lives inside. Does anyone want to make a guess?"

4. Call on students to make up the words for each page as the class "reads" the book together.

5. As the class tells the story, hold up picture cards as new words come up in the story to make a real-life connection between the words and the story. For example, when you get to the page where the character is making butter, hold up the butter card.

6. Stop reading at page 20. (In the picture, the character is walking back to her cottage with the syrup in her hand thinking about all the steps she has done to make the pancakes.) Have students predict what will happen next by drawing or writing in their journals. Students will need to make a prediction and use their inference skills to guess what will happen next.

7. Have students discuss their prediction with a partner. This will allow English learners (ELs) to hear their peers' ideas while sharing their own ideas with one other person in case they are too shy to share with the whole class.

8. Have students who are willing share their ideas with the whole class.

Assessment

Students will draw or write their prediction of the story and explain it.

Additional Resources

Related Websites

Games students could play for follow-up discussions and a chance to build their own pancakes and serve them in a restaurant—

- www.coolmath-games.com/0-papas-pancakeria/
- www.agame.com/game/pancake-bar.

Inferring practice on the Into the Book website; click on Inferring (magnifying glass): http://reading.ecb.org/student/entry.html?login=.

Related Apps

- Pancake Maker (free)—use the ingredients to make your own pancakes and decorate them, too. Available on iTunes.
- Pan Cake Maker (free)—pretend to make pancakes. Available on Google play.
- Inference Ace (free for level 1)—practice making inferences. Available on Google play and iTunes.

Further Reading

Kim, D. (2009). Working with texts to develop ESOL reading strategies. In L. Savova (Ed.), *Effective use of textbooks* (pp. 109–117). Alexandra, VA: TESOL. Retrieved from http://www.tesol.org/docs/books/bk_CP _usingtextbooks_592.

TESOL PreK–12 English Language Proficiency Standards

Standard 1: English language learners communicate for social, intercultural, and instructional purposes within the school setting.

Standard 2: English language learners communicate information, ideas, and concepts necessary for academic success in the area of language arts.

Common Core State Standards ELA Suggested Connections

The following are the Common Core State Standards for English Language Arts that are aligned with this lesson. The rubric on the next page includes a sampling of grade levels to show how the standards get more complex at higher grade levels.

Writing: W.K.3; W.1.3; W.2.3; W.3.3

Speaking and Listening: SL.K.4; SL.1.4; SL.2.4; SL.3.4

PANCAKES FOR BREAKFAST

CCSS Sample Rubric

Go to www.tesol.org/wordless to complete the rubric by adding your grade level standards from the Common Core website.

Writing: http://www.corestandards.org/ELA-Literacy/W/introduction/

Speaking and Listening: http://www.corestandards.org/ELA-Literacy/SL/introduction/

	Grading Criteria			
	Outstanding 10	**Adequate 8–9**	**Developing 1–7**	**Not Present 0**
	All of the criteria are present and fully developed.	Most of the criteria are present and adequately developed.	Some of the criteria are present and somewhat developed.	None of the criteria are present.
Standards	**Teacher's Comments**			
W.K.3. Use a combination of drawing, dictating, and writing to narrate a single event or several loosely linked events, tell about the events in the order in which they occurred, and provide a reaction to what happened.				
SL.K.4. Describe familiar people, places, things, and events and, with prompting and support, provide additional detail. *or*				
W.3.3. Write narratives to develop real or imagined experiences or events using effective technique, descriptive details, and clear event sequences.				

(continued)

	Grading Criteria			
	Outstanding 10	**Adequate 8–9**	**Developing 1–7**	**Not Present 0**
	All of the criteria are present and fully developed.	Most of the criteria are present and adequately developed.	Some of the criteria are present and somewhat developed.	None of the criteria are present.
Standards	Teacher's Comments			
SL.3.4. Report on a topic or text, tell a story, or recount an experience with appropriate facts and relevant, descriptive details, speaking clearly at an understandable pace.				
Total points				

CARL AT THE DOG SHOW

by Alexandra Day

Lesson by Christine M. Bowen-Kreiner

Level	Beginning
Preparation Time	5 minutes
Length of Lesson	50 minutes
Objective	Students will identify their favorite part of the story and share it orally as well as in writing.

Materials
- *Carl at the Dog Show* by Alexandra Day (New York, NY: Little Simon, 2012)
- Writing paper with prompt prewritten or prompt on the board for students to copy
- Dry-erase board and marker
- Crayons and pencils

Vocabulary
- champion
- dog show
- grooming
- heaviest
- longest
- ribbon
- shortest
- trick

Procedure

1. Explain to students that they will be reading the story *Carl at the Dog Show* and writing about their favorite part of the book. To begin the lesson, complete a brief picture walk, showing the students all of the pictures briefly, to expose the students to the story.

2. Next, go through the story to allow students to see the illustrations and gain an understanding about what is happening in the beginning, middle, and end.

3. After reading the text, think aloud, and state your favorite part of the text, for example, "My favorite part was when the girl dressed the dog in a costume. I liked this part because it made me laugh!" After providing an example, have students turn and talk to a buddy for 1 minute to discuss their favorite parts of the story and why they liked them. This will allow EL students to use language with a peer. Have a plan in place to pair EL students with students who demonstrate higher levels of English to support language needs. Then ask for volunteers to share their ideas to the whole group while charting the ideas on the board. Tell the students that when giving an opinion, they should include their favorite part of the story, information about why they liked it, and how they felt at the end. A picture can also be created to help express ideas and facilitate language. Based on a student's level, use your professional judgment to differentiate the sentence requirements.

4. After the students have talked about their favorite parts, use one of the examples given by the students to generate a model sentence on the board for the students to see. Use the prompt, "My favorite part of the story was when . . . ." For example: "My favorite part of the story was when the girl dressed the dog in a pretty bow. I liked it because it made me laugh!" As students work to create their own sentence in a whole-group format, allow them to volunteer to share their thoughts on the spelling of the words. After the sentence is generated, provide the correct spelling of the words, thus allowing the students to feel validated in their attempts to sound out the words as they write, as well as see the correct formation of the words in English.

5. Finally, have students return to their seats to complete the following prompt: My favorite part of the story was when . . . . For students who need additional scaffolding or prompts, provide students with sample choices from the text. Rotate throughout the groups to provide support and scribe as needed.

Assessment

Students' writing will show if they were able to share their favorite part of the story. Anecdotal notes could also be recorded to show speaking skills.

Additional Resources

Related Websites

- Additional reading ideas using the theme of dogs—www.pinterest.com /search/pins/?q=dogs%20books%20for%20kids.
- Video example of related books about Carl the dog available at Carolyn Cart's website, Storytime Standouts—www.storytimestandouts.com/2012/06/18 /picture-books-best/good-dog-carl-wordless-picture-book/.

Related Apps

- I Like Dogs: Dog Picture Book for Kids (free)—e-book about dogs. Available on iTunes.
- Perfect Dog HD Free: Ultimate Breed Guide to Dogs (free)—learn about various dog breeds. Available on iTunes and Google play.

Further Reading

Cheri, W., & Pilonietta, P. (2012). Using interactive writing instruction with kindergarten and first-grade English language learners. *Early Childhood Education Journal, 40,* 145–150.

TESOL PreK–12 English Language Proficiency Standards

Standard 1: English language learners communicate for social, intercultural, and instructional purposes within the school setting.

Standard 2: English language learners communicate information, ideas, and concepts necessary for academic success in the area of language arts.

Common Core State Standards ELA Suggested Connections

The following are the Common Core State Standards for English Language Arts that are aligned with this lesson. The rubric on the next page includes a sampling of grade levels to show how the standards get more complex at higher grade levels.

Writing: W.K.1; W.1.1

K.1. Use a combination of drawing, dictating, and writing to compose opinion pieces in which they tell a reader the topic or the name of the book they are writing about and state an opinion or preference about the topic or book (e.g., My favorite book is . . .).

1.1. Write opinion pieces in which they introduce the topic or name the book they are writing about, state an opinion, supply a reason for the opinion, and provide some sense of closure.

Speaking and Listening: SL.K.6; SL.1.6

K.6. Speak audibly and express thoughts, feelings, and ideas clearly.

1.6. Produce complete sentences when appropriate to task and situation.

CARL AT THE DOG SHOW

CCSS Sample Rubric

Go to www.tesol.org/wordless to complete the rubric by adding your grade level standards from the Common Core website.

Writing: http://www.corestandards.org/ELA-Literacy/W/introduction/

Speaking and Listening: http://www.corestandards.org/ELA-Literacy/SL/introduction/

	Grading Criteria			
	Outstanding 10	**Adequate 8–9**	**Developing 1–7**	**Not Present 0**
	All of the criteria are present and fully developed.	Most of the criteria are present and adequately developed.	Some of the criteria are present and somewhat developed.	None of the criteria are present.
Standards	**Teacher's Comments**			
W.K.1. Use a combination of drawing, dictating, and writing to compose opinion pieces in which they tell a reader the topic or the name of the book they are writing about and state an opinion or preference about the topic or book.				
SL.K.6. Speak audibly and express thoughts, feelings, and ideas clearly in a sentence(s). *or*				
W.1.1. Write opinion pieces in which they introduce the topic or name the book they are writing about, state an opinion, supply a reason for the opinion, and provide some sense of closure.				

(continued)	Grading Criteria			
	Outstanding 10	**Adequate 8–9**	**Developing 1–7**	**Not Present 0**
	All of the criteria are present and fully developed.	Most of the criteria are present and adequately developed.	Some of the criteria are present and somewhat developed.	None of the criteria are present.
Standards	**Teacher's Comments**			
SL.1.6. Produce complete sentences when appropriate to task and situation.				
Total points				

GOOD DOG, CARL

by Alexandra Day

Lesson by Christine Bowen-Kreiner

Level	Beginning
Preparation Time	5 minutes
Length of Lesson	50 minutes
Objective	Students will understand the meaning and relationship of the illustrations in the text and the story. For more advanced learners, students will use the illustrations in the text to describe the setting, character, and events in a story.

Materials

- *Good Dog, Carl* by Alexandra Day (New York, NY: Little Simon, 1996)
- 10 brown bags
- 10 sets of prewritten note cards with the listed terms
- Note-taking sheets to record anecdotal notes on students

Vocabulary

- clean
- climb
- dance
- eat
- jump
- run
- swim

Procedure

1. State the objective of the Lesson by explaining to students that they will be reading the story *Good Dog, Carl* to learn how the different pictures in the story help the reader understand the plot, as well as how the different illustrations represent various action words. To begin the lesson, complete a brief picture walk to expose the students to the story.

2. Next, go through the story to allow students to see the illustrations and understand what is happening in the beginning, middle, and end. Point out the different types of actions demonstrated by the dog and the baby. The action words referenced in the lesson include run, jump, dance, climb, swim, eat, and clean. When pointing out the action words, think aloud and explain that even though there are not words in the book, the pictures illustrate what is happening from page to page in the story. When the pictures are put in order, from left to right and top to bottom, the reader can follow along what is happening in each scene of the story. Provide an example of this action by referencing the page in which Carl the dog is dancing near the radio. Using this example, point out the vocabulary you see in the picture that lets you know the dog is dancing. You can also act out how you might dance if you were a character in the story.

3. After reading the text, ask students how the pictures helped them understand what was happening in the story. Allow students to turn and talk to a peer to describe how the pictures helped them understand the story. Ahead of time, plan to pair beginning EL students with students who demonstrate higher levels of English to support language needs. Provide visuals if needed, or use the website Speaking of Speech.com (www.speakingofspeech.com) to gain additional visuals. After students have turned and talked, call on volunteers to share their ideas on how the illustrations helped them understand what was going on in the story.

4. After students have talked about how the illustrations helped them understand Carl babysitting, have students look at the book on the overhead projector. During this whole-group time, go to the page where Carl is dancing, and have students describe the action being displayed on the page. Provide answer choices for the whole group to select from to help them key in on specific vocabulary terms (e.g., dance, clean, eat). Write three options on the board, and have students turn and talk to one another to decide which action verb was being displayed on the given page. After students have talked with their peers, call on students to share their answers. After students have completed the selected page, do the same for the remaining actions in the book. Give answer choices (run, jump, dance, climb, swim, eat, and clean), or fade back the scaffolds as necessary.

5. After going through the specific actions in the whole-group setting, have students split up and go with their partners back to their seats. When students are in their seats, pass out the brown paper bags and a set of index cards with the verbs from the story listed on them, one verb on each card

(write the words on the cards ahead of time). Give one bag and one set of cards to each pair of students and have students put the cards in the bag. During this time, pick two students to model how to play the following action-verb game.

6. Have one of the volunteers pull a card from the bag and act out the verb; the other student tries to guess what it is. Begin the activity, having one student of each pair pull a card out of the bag and keep it out of sight of the other student. The student who pulls the card from the bag will perform the action listed on the card, while the other student uses a sentence to state what the other person is doing. If the student has trouble reading the word, the teacher should provide support as needed. For example, if a girl pulls the card "jump," the girl will jump up and down. The other student will try to determine what the girl is doing and state, "The girl jumps." The sentence can be expanded based on student ability level and age. For students just learning the vocabulary terms, the teacher can have the student simply identify the action with a one-word response instead of a full sentence. Students should alternate back and forth until all the cards are used up. During this time, the teacher should be walking around to take anecdotal notes on students' ability to identify and use the verbs while speaking.

Assessment

Anecdotal notes should be taken during the lesson to gain information on the student's ability to understand how the illustrations support the story. Notes should also be taken as the students complete the verb game.

Additional Resources

Related Websites

Additional reading ideas to teach verbs—www.eslkidstuff.com/esl-kids-games/action-games.htm#.U5ZPbOddVQc.

Additional ideas on teaching verbs—www.pinterest.com/search/pins/?q=verb%20games.

Related Apps

- Action in Video Lite (free)—provides interactive videos to match verbs and objects. Available on iTunes.
- Action Words (free)—provides audio and visuals to match photographs with simple verbs. Available on iTunes.

Further Reading

Flood, J., & Lapp, D. (1997). Literacy instruction for students acquiring English: Moving beyond the immersion debate. San Diego, CA: Reading Teacher.

TESOL PreK–12 English Language Proficiency Standards

Standard 2: English language learners communicate information, ideas, and concepts necessary for academic success in the area of language arts.

Common Core State Standards ELA Suggested Connections

The following are the Common Core State Standards for English Language Arts that are aligned with this lesson. The rubric on the next page includes a sampling of grade levels to show how the standards get more complex at higher grade levels.

Reading: RL.K.7; RL.1.7; RL.2.7

GOOD DOG, CARL

CCSS Sample Rubric

Go to www.tesol.org/wordless to complete the rubric by adding your grade level standards from the Common Core website.

Reading: http://www.corestandards.org/ELA-Literacy/RL/introduction-for-k-5/

Standards	Grading Criteria			
	Outstanding 10	**Adequate 8–9**	**Developing 1–7**	**Not Present 0**
	All of the criteria are present and fully developed.	Most of the criteria are present and adequately developed.	Some of the criteria are present and somewhat developed.	None of the criteria are present.
Standards	**Teacher's Comments**			
RL.K.7. With prompting and support, describe the relationship between illustrations and the story in which they appear (e.g., what moment in a story an illustration depicts). *or*				
RL.1.7 Use illustrations and details in a story to describe its characters, setting, or events. *or*				
RL.2.7 Use information gained from the illustrations and words in a print or digital text to demonstrate understanding of its characters, setting, or plot.				
Total points				

WAVE

by Suzy Lee

Lesson by Jessica Karbassi

Level	Beginning to intermediate
Preparation Time	5 minutes
Length of Lesson	60 minutes
Objectives	1. Students will use a combination of drawing, dictating, and writing to communicate information and ideas about a given topic.
	2. Students will participate in collaborative conversations with partners or in small groups about a common topic.

Materials

- *Wave* by Suzy Lee (San Francisco, CA: Chronicle Books, 2008)
- Camera
- Paper and pencils
- Emotion words printed out with picture cues (with a student friendly definition)
- Computer

Vocabulary

- contemplative
- content
- curious
- ecstatic

- ferocious
- fierce
- hesitant
- joyful
- thrilled
- timid

Procedure

1. Do a picture walk through the entire book, page by page, so students can see what happens throughout the story.

2. Do a second picture walk, this time discussing what is happening on each page with the students. With the students, discuss what they think the girl in the story is thinking and feeling on each page. Have students label each page with a different emotion. Encourage students go beyond common emotion words such as happy or sad. Offer emotion words (already printed out with a picture cue) if the students are having a difficult time thinking of more complex emotion vocabulary.

3. Divide the class into groups. Give each group a bag of emotion words. Inside each bag should be related words and synonyms for an emotion. Students then sort the words from one extreme to another. For example students may receive a bag with the words "content," "glad," "happy," "joyful," "thrilled," and "ecstatic." Students discuss these words and then sort the words from one extreme to another. Consider giving students the two end words; for example, tell students to sort the words from "content" to "ecstatic."

4. Ask students to write about a situation in which they might feel a particular emotion. For example, if a student chooses to write about the word "timid," he or she will write about a time he or she felt timid.

5. Take a photograph that depicts what each student wrote about. This picture will be included with the writing in a class book. For example, if a student wrote, "I feel timid when I am asked to speak in front of the whole class," then take a picture of the student standing in front of the class.

6. Put all the students' writing and pictures in a class book. If the resources are available, have students type their responses on the computer and assist them in inserting their pictures into the document.

Assessment

Students' writing can be used to determine if they were able to communicate information or ideas in writing. Students' speaking and listening skills can be observed during the group discussions.

Additional Resources

Related Websites

Brief clip of waves crashing on shore (could be shown prior to reading the story, especially important for students who may have never visited the beach)—www.youtube.com/watch?v=LfsQbYfwi-I.

Science video on ocean currents—www.brainpop.com/science/earthsystem/oceancurrents/preview.weml.

Related Apps

- Where's My Water (free or $1.99)—complete physics-based puzzles to cut through dirt to get to fresh water. Available on iTunes and Google play.
- Nemo's Reef (free)—create your own reef. Available on iTunes and Google play.

Further Reading

River, J. (2013). *How do you feel today? A kids book about feelings and emotions.* Kindle Direct. Available at http://www.amazon.com/Emotions-Feelings -feel-today-about ebook/dp/B00DP3Z4YG.

TESOL PreK–12 English Language Proficiency Standards

Standard 1: English language learners communicate for social, intercultural, and instructional purposes within the school setting.

Standard 2: English language learners communicate information, ideas, and concepts necessary for academic success in the area of language arts.

Common Core State Standards ELA Suggested Connections

The following are the Common Core State Standards for English Language Arts that are aligned with this lesson. The rubric on the next page includes a sampling of grade levels to show how the standards get more complex at higher grade levels.

Writing: W.K.1; W.1.1; W.2.1; W.3.1

K.1. Use a combination of drawing, dictating, and writing to compose opinion pieces in which they tell a reader the topic or the name of the book they are writing about and state an opinion or preference about the topic or book (e.g., *My favorite book is . . .*).

3.1. Write opinion pieces on topics or texts, supporting a point of view with reasons.

Speaking and Listening: SL.K.1; SL.1.1; SL.2.1; SL.3.1

K.1. Participate in collaborative conversations with diverse partners about *kindergarten topics and texts* with peers and adults in small and larger groups.

3.1. Engage effectively in a range of collaborative conversations (one-on-one, in groups, and teacher-led) with diverse partners on *grade 3 topics and texts,* building on others' ideas and expressing their own clearly.

WAVE

CCSS Sample Rubric

Go to www.tesol.org/wordless to complete the rubric by adding your grade level standards from the Common Core website.

Writing: http://www.corestandards.org/ELA-Literacy/W/introduction/

Speaking and Listening: http://www.corestandards.org/ELA-Literacy/SL /introduction/

	Grading Criteria			
	Outstanding 10	**Adequate 8–9**	**Developing 1–7**	**Not Present 0**
	All of the criteria are present and fully developed.	Most of the criteria are present and adequately developed.	Some of the criteria are present and somewhat developed.	None of the criteria are present.
Standards	**Teacher's Comments**			
W.K.1. Use a combination of drawing, dictating, and writing to compose opinion pieces in which they tell a reader the topic or the name of the book they are writing about and state an opinion or preference about the topic or book (e.g., *My favorite book is . . .*).				
SL.K.1. Participate in collaborative conversations with diverse partners about *kindergarten topics and texts* with peers and adults in small and larger groups. a. Follow agreed-upon rules for discussions (e.g., listening to others and taking turns speaking about the topics and texts under discussion). *or*				

(continued)	Grading Criteria			
	Outstanding 10	**Adequate 8–9**	**Developing 1–7**	**Not Present 0**
	All of the criteria are present and fully developed.	Most of the criteria are present and adequately developed.	Some of the criteria are present and somewhat developed.	None of the criteria are present.
Standards	**Teacher's Comments**			
W.3.1. Write opinion pieces on topics or texts, supporting a point of view with reasons.				
SL.3.1. Engage effectively in a range of collaborative conversations (one-on-one, in groups, and teacher-led) with diverse partners on *grade 3 topics and texts*, building on others' ideas and expressing their own clearly.				
Total points				

RAINSTORM

by Barbara Lehman

Lesson by Jessica S. Cohen

Level	Beginning to intermediate
Preparation Time	5 minutes
Length of Lesson	45 minutes
Objective	Students will write questions to ask a peer in an interview and conduct the interview. They will also answer interview questions themselves.

Materials

- *Rainstorm* by Barbara Lehman (Boston, MA: Houghton Mifflin, 2007)
- Toy microphones
- Paper and pencils
- Journal
- Chart paper or document camera
- Video camera (optional)

Vocabulary

- chest
- island
- ladder
- lighthouse
- lonely
- stormy

Procedure

1. Ask students to talk about things they like to do on a rainy day. This will help them generate background knowledge and start thinking about the context of the story.

2. Show students the book *Rainstorm.* Demonstrate how to tell a story by using the pictures. Show each page and call on students to describe what they think is happening in the story based on the pictures. You can jump in and add important details that the students may leave out or ask questions to help support students' telling of the story.

3. Ask students to imagine that they had the chance to meet the boy in this story. Encourage them to think of some questions they would like to ask the boy in this story. The questions could be about how he was feeling, what he saw, and so forth. Record the questions on chart paper.

4. Have students record a few more questions in their writing journals.

5. After students come up with their questions, pair up the students. Have students take turns being the "newscaster" and the "main character" and ask and answer each other's questions. The number of interview questions asked and answered can be based on the child's English proficiency.

6. Last, students conduct their interviews in front of the class or record their interviews using a video camera and create movies of their newscast.

Assessment

The students' journals with their written questions will be reviewed, and their speaking skills while conducting the interviews and answering questions will be observed.

Additional Resources

Additional Books about Rain

The Puddle by David McPhail (New York, NY: Farrar, Straus and Giroux, 2000).

Thundercake by Patricia Polacco (Boston, MA: Houghton Mifflin, 1997).

Related Websites

Videos about how rain is formed—

*   http://pbskids.org/video/?category=Sid%20the%20Science%20Kid&pid =F451nFU8zKqDn50X0d_qdH85ZUfR7gx_.
*   www.brainpopjr.com/science/weather/watercycle/preview.weml.

Related Apps

*   My Story—School Edition ($3.99)—create your own book. Draw pictures and use stamps or import photos to go along with the stories. Students could create stories about their rainy day adventures. Available on iTunes.

- Kids Weather ($1.99)—check out videos and radar in this weather app for children. Available on iTunes and Google play.

Further Reading

Branley, F. M. (1983). *Down comes the rain.* New York, NY: HarperCollins.

TESOL PreK–12 English Language Proficiency Standards

Standard 1: English language learners communicate for social, intercultural, and instructional purposes within the school setting.

Standard 2: English language learners communicate information, ideas, and concepts necessary for academic success in the area of language arts.

Common Core State Standards ELA Suggested Connections

The following are the Common Core State Standards for English Language Arts that are aligned with this lesson. The rubric on the next page includes a sampling of grade levels to show how the standards get more complex at higher grade levels.

Reading: RL.1.1; RL.2.1; RL.3.1

Speaking and Listening: SL.1.3; SL.2.3; SL.3.3

RAINSTORM

CCSS Sample Rubric

Go to www.tesol.org/wordless to complete the rubric by adding your grade level standards from the Common Core website.

Reading: http://www.corestandards.org/ELA-Literacy/RL/introduction-for-k-5/

Speaking and Listening: http://www.corestandards.org/ELA-Literacy/SL/introduction/

	Grading Criteria			
	Outstanding 10	**Adequate 8–9**	**Developing 1–7**	**Not Present 0**
	All of the criteria are present and fully developed.	Most of the criteria are present and adequately developed.	Some of the criteria are present and somewhat developed.	None of the criteria are present.
Standards	**Teacher's Comments**			
RL.1.1. Ask and answer questions about key details in a text.				
SL.1.3. Ask and answer questions about what a speaker says in order to gather additional information or clarify something that is not understood. *or*				
RL.3.1. Ask and answer questions to demonstrate understanding of a text, referring explicitly to the text as the basis for the answers.				
SL.3.3. Ask and answer questions about information from a speaker, offering appropriate elaboration and detail.				
Total points				

MY FRIEND RABBIT

by Eric Rohmann

Lesson by Malerie E. Rubnitz

Level	Intermediate to advanced
Preparation Time	5 minutes
Length of Lesson	45 minutes
Objective	Students will write dialogue for different parts of the story in order to sequence the events and create a beginning, a middle, and an end. They will then have a discussion about their completed stories.

Materials

- *My Friend Rabbit* by Eric Rohmann (New York, NY: Square Fish, 2002)
- Chart paper
- Sticky notes
- Markers

Vocabulary

- airplane
- annoy
- friend
- frustrated
- hefty
- peering
- rabbit
- soaring

Procedure

1. Introduce the book to students by reading aloud the title and author's name. Inform the students that they will be working in small groups to write dialogue for different parts of the story.

2. Read the first three pages of the story and model thinking about how to add dialogue to the characters. Then write down the dialogue on sticky notes and place them on the pages where they belong in the story.

3. Have students participate in a jigsaw activity. They will form home-base groups and then break up into specific groups that focus on writing dialogue for three to four pages of the book. The students will use sticky notes to add dialogue to their assigned pages.

4. Students work with their home-base groups to put all the dialogue together for the entire book. They put all their sticky notes into the book to complete the story. The students will discuss how to connect all the dialogue to create a clear beginning, middle, and end to the story.

Assessment

The students' written dialogue for their part of the story will be reviewed, and their speaking skills while discussing their completed stories will be observed.

Additional Resources

Related Websites

BrainPOP video about writing with dialogue—www.brainpop.com/english /writing/dialogue/preview.weml.

A site where students can create their own comics to practice writing stories with dialogue—www.readwritethink.org/parent-afterschool-resources /games-tools/comic-creator-a-30237.html.

Related Apps

- Story Wheel ($2.99)—write stories and record your voice on an iPad. Available on iTunes.
- Toontastic (free)—create cartoons and stories and record your voice on an iPad. Available on iTunes.

Further Reading

Bell, J. S. (2014). *The 7 tools of dialogue*. Retrieved from http://www.writers digest.com/online-editor/the-7-tools-of-dialogue.

TESOL PreK–12 English Language Proficiency Standards

Standard 1: English language learners communicate for social, intercultural, and instructional purposes within the school setting.

Standard 2: English language learners communicate information, ideas, and concepts necessary for academic success in the area of language arts.

Common Core State Standards ELA Suggested Connections

The following are the Common Core State Standards for English Language Arts that are aligned with this lesson. The rubric on the next page includes a sampling of grade levels to show how the standards get more complex at higher grade levels.

Writing: W.3.3; W.4.3; W.5.3; W.6.3; W.7.3; W.8.3; W.9–10.3; W.11–12.3

Speaking and Listening: SL.3.4; SL.4.4; SL.5.4; SL.6.4; SL.7.4; SL.8.4; SL.9–10.4; SL.11–12.4

MY FRIEND RABBIT

CCSS Sample Rubric

Go to www.tesol.org/wordless to complete the rubric by adding your grade level standards from the Common Core website.

Writing: http://www.corestandards.org/ELA-Literacy/W/introduction/

Speaking and Listening: http://www.corestandards.org/ELA-Literacy/SL /introduction/

	Grading Criteria			
	Outstanding 10	**Adequate 8–9**	**Developing 1–7**	**Not Present 0**
	All of the criteria are present and fully developed.	Most of the criteria are present and adequately developed.	Some of the criteria are present and somewhat developed.	None of the criteria are present.
Standards	**Teacher's Comments**			
W.3.3. Write narratives to develop real or imagined experiences or events using effective technique, descriptive details, and clear event sequences.				
SL.3.4. Report on a topic or text, tell a story, or recount an experience with appropriate facts and relevant, descriptive details, speaking clearly at an understandable pace. *or*				
W.6.3. Write narratives to develop real or imagined experiences or events using effective technique, relevant descriptive details, and well-structured event sequences.				

(continued)	Grading Criteria			
	Outstanding 10	**Adequate 8–9**	**Developing 1–7**	**Not Present 0**
	All of the criteria are present and fully developed.	Most of the criteria are present and adequately developed.	Some of the criteria are present and somewhat developed.	None of the criteria are present.
Standards	**Teacher's Comments**			
SL.6.4. Present claims and findings, sequencing ideas logically and using pertinent descriptions, facts, and details to accentuate main ideas or themes; use appropriate eye contact, adequate volume, and clear pronunciation. *or*				
W.11–12.3. Write narratives to develop real or imagined experiences or events using effective technique, well-chosen details, and well-structured event sequences.				
SL.11–12.4. Present information, findings, and supporting evidence, conveying a clear and distinct perspective, such that listeners can follow the line of reasoning, alternative or opposing perspectives are addressed, and the organization, development, substance, and style are appropriate to purpose, audience, and a range of formal and informal tasks.				
Total points				

A BOY, A DOG, AND A FROG

by Mercer Mayer

Lesson by Monica E. Cortada

Level	Beginning to advanced
Preparation Time	5 minutes
Length of Lesson	30–50 minutes
Objective	Students will use prepositional phrases and props to retell a story.

Materials

- *A Boy, a Dog and a Frog* by Mercer Mayer (New York, NY: Dial Books for Young Readers, 1967)
- Picture of the boy, dog, and frog from the story
- Blue paper to serve as the pond
- Green paper for lily pads
- Brown paper for the tree trunk
- Small tea strainer with handle to serve as the net
- Paper footprints
- Cards with prepositional phrases required to tell the story (e.g., down the _____, over the _____, in the _____, on top of _____, across the _____)

Vocabulary

- boy
- branch
- bucket
- caught
- dog

- fell
- frog
- lonely
- net
- ran
- sad
- tripped
- water
- went

Procedure

1. Read the story to the students and show the cards with the prepositional phrases as they appear in the story.
2. While reading, have students hold up the props as the words are mentioned.
3. With the students in pairs, have the linguistically stronger student retell the story first, using props and the prepositional phrases modeled. Then, have students switch roles.
4. After the retelling, let the pairs of students make up their own stories while using the prepositional phrases. These new stories can be written, videoed, and turned into class films.

Assessment

The teacher will informally observe students' oral responses using prepositional phrases during the retellings. However, before beginning the lesson the teacher could record one or two students trying to tell the story without support, then rerecord them retelling after the lesson to note language growth. All the students' written stories (and videos) will be reviewed to check if they were able to use prepositional phrases correctly.

Additional Resources

Related Websites

Resources from the publisher of the book—www.teachingbooks.net/tb .cgi?tid=970.

A wordless video of a pond habitat—www.youtube.com/watch?v=rYk NYUI4nD0.

A more detailed video of the pond ecosystem—www.youtube.com/watch?v =kMBGd9FL9_A.

Related Apps

- Phrasal Verbs Machine by Cambridge University Press (free)—available for iOS and Android.

- iMovie and GarageBand ($4.99)—turn student stories into movies with custom soundtracks. Available on iTunes.

References for Further Reading:

Wright, A. (1989). *Pictures for language learning.* New York, NY: Cambridge University Press.

The complete Frog series in order—

1. Mayer, M. (1969). *Frog, where are you?* New York, NY: Dial Press.
2. Mayer, M., & Mayer, M. (1971). *A boy, a dog, a frog, and a friend.* New York, NY: Dial Press.
3. Mayer, M. (1973). *Frog on his own.* New York, NY: Dial Press.
4. Mayer, M. (1974). *Frog goes to dinner.* New York, NY: Dial Press.
5. Mayer, M., & Mayer, M. (1975). *One frog too many.* New York, NY: Dial Press.

TESOL PreK–12 English Language Proficiency Standards

Standard 1: English language learners communicate for social, intercultural, and instructional purposes within the school setting.

Standard 2: English language learners communicate information, ideas, and concepts necessary for academic success in the area of language arts.

Common Core State Standards ELA Suggested Connections

The following are the Common Core State Standards for English Language Arts that are aligned with this lesson. The rubric on the next page includes a sampling of grade levels to show how the standards get more complex at higher grade levels.

Writing: W.K.3; W.1.3; W.2.3; W.3.3; W.4.3; W.5.3; W.6.3; W.7.3; W.8.3; W.9–10.3; W.11–12.3

Speaking and Listening: SL.K.4; SL.1.4; SL.2.4; SL.3.4; SL.4.4; SL.5.4; SL.6.4; SL.7.4; SL.8.4; SL.9–10.4; SL.11–12.4

A BOY, A DOG, AND A FROG

CCSS Sample Rubric

Go to www.tesol.org/wordless to complete the rubric by adding your grade level standards from the Common Core website.

Writing: http://www.corestandards.org/ELA-Literacy/W/introduction/

Speaking and Listening: http://www.corestandards.org/ELA-Literacy/SL /introduction/

	Grading Criteria			
	Outstanding 10	**Adequate 8–9**	**Developing 1–7**	**Not Present 0**
	All of the criteria are present and fully developed.	Most of the criteria are present and adequately developed.	Some of the criteria are present and somewhat developed.	None of the criteria are present.
Standards	**Teacher's Comments**			
W.K.3. Use a combination of pointing, dictating, and writing to narrate a single event or several loosely linked events, tell about the events in the order in which they occurred, and provide a reaction to what happened.				
SL.K.4. Describe familiar people, places, things, and events and, with prompting and support, provide additional detail. *or*				
W.6.3. Write narratives to develop real or imagined experiences or events using effective technique, relevant descriptive details, and well-structured event sequences. *or*				

(continued)	Grading Criteria			
	Outstanding 10	**Adequate 8–9**	**Developing 1–7**	**Not Present 0**
	All of the criteria are present and fully developed.	Most of the criteria are present and adequately developed.	Some of the criteria are present and somewhat developed.	None of the criteria are present.
Standards	**Teacher's Comments**			
SL.6.4. Present findings, sequencing ideas logically and using pertinent descriptions, facts, and details to accentuate main ideas or themes; use appropriate eye contact, adequate volume, and clear pronunciation. *or*				
W.11–12.3. Write narratives to develop real or imagined experiences or events using effective technique, well-chosen details, and well-structured event sequences.				
SL.11–12.4. Present information, findings, and supporting evidence, conveying a clear and distinct perspective, such that listeners can follow the line of reasoning, alternative or opposing perspectives are addressed, and the organization, development, substance, and style are appropriate to purpose, audience, and a range of formal and informal tasks.				
Total points				

CHALK

by Bill Thomson

Lesson by Gilda Martinez-Alba

Level	Beginning to advanced
Preparation Time	5 minutes
Length of Lesson	50 minutes
Objective	The students will write scripts to the story and will read and act out the scripts to make a movie.

Materials
- *Chalk* by Bill Thompson (New York, NY: Amazon Children's Publishing, 2010)
- Chalk
- Paper and pencils
- Video camera
- Computer

Vocabulary
- butterflies
- chalk
- dinosaur
- raincoats
- rainy
- relieved
- scary
- sun
- umbrellas
- walking

Procedure

1. Do a relatively quick picture walk, going through the entire book page by page, so students can see what happens in the beginning, middle, and end of the story.

2. Give students time to write down what they believe is happening, as if they were the author of the book telling the story, while slowly going through the pages. Beginning ELs could write down a few words to capture the beginning, middle, and end of the story; whereas more advanced ELs could add in details such as about the characters and events. Students could write on paper or on the computer, depending on the resources available.

3. Have students re-create the story. In other words, the students would practice their lines and act out the story.

4. Last, using video editing software, create a polished film, a movie based on the book, with students who are interested playing the parts.

Assessment

The students' written scripts will be reviewed and their speaking skills while acting out the scripts will be observed.

Additional Resources

Related Websites

Artist Julian Beever's website has amazing 3D sidewalk chalk drawings that could be used for follow-up discussions—www.boredpanda.com /44-amazing-3d-sidewalk-chalk-artworks-by-julian-beever/.

Pinterest page with chalk illusions—www.pinterest.com/michelle816 /chalk-illusions/.

Pinterest page with numerous ideas for sidewalk chalk activities—www .pinterest.com/handsonaswegrow/sidewalk-chalk-activities/.

Related Apps

- Hello Chalk (free)—draw with "chalk" on an iPad.
- Art of Glow (free)—draw with bright, glowing colors on an iPad.

Further Reading

Tomas, Z., Kostka, I., & Mott-Smith, J. A. (2013). *Teaching writing*. Alexandria, VA: TESOL International Association.

TESOL PreK–12 English Language Proficiency Standards

Standard 1: English language learners communicate for social, intercultural, and instructional purposes within the school setting.

Standard 2: English language learners communicate information, ideas, and concepts necessary for academic success in the area of language arts.

Common Core State Standards ELA Suggested Connections

The following are the Common Core State Standards for English Language Arts that are aligned with this lesson. The rubric on the next page includes a sampling of grade levels to show how the standards get more complex at higher grade levels.

Writing: W.K.3; W.1.3; W.2.3; W.3.3; W.4.3; W.5.3; W.6.3; W.7.3; W.8.3; W.9–10.3; W.11–12.3

Speaking and Listening: SL.K.4; SL.1.4; SL.2.4; SL.3.4; SL.4.4; SL.5.4; SL.6.4; SL.7.4; SL.8.4; SL.9–10.4; SL.11–12.4

CHALK

CCSS Sample Rubric

Go to www.tesol.org/wordless to complete the rubric by adding your grade level standards from the Common Core website.

Writing: http://www.corestandards.org/ELA-Literacy/W/introduction/

Speaking and Listening: http://www.corestandards.org/ELA-Literacy/SL/introduction/

	Grading Criteria			
	Outstanding 10	**Adequate 8–9**	**Developing 1–7**	**Not Present 0**
	All of the criteria are present and fully developed.	Most of the criteria are present and adequately developed.	Some of the criteria are present and somewhat developed.	None of the criteria are present.
Standards	**Teacher's Comments**			
W.K.3. Use a combination of drawing, dictating, and writing to narrate a single event or several loosely linked events, tell about the events in the order in which they occurred, and provide a reaction to what happened.				
SL.K.4. Describe familiar people, places, things, and events and, with prompting and support, provide additional detail. *or*				
W.6.3 Write narratives to develop real or imagined experiences or events using effective technique, relevant descriptive details, and well-structured event sequences.				

(continued)	Grading Criteria			
	Outstanding 10	**Adequate 8–9**	**Developing 1–7**	**Not Present 0**
	All of the criteria are present and fully developed.	Most of the criteria are present and adequately developed.	Some of the criteria are present and somewhat developed.	None of the criteria are present.
Standards	**Teacher's Comments**			
SL.6.4. Present claims and findings, sequencing ideas logically and using pertinent descriptions, facts, and details to accentuate main ideas or themes; use appropriate eye contact, adequate volume, and clear pronunciation. *or*				
W.11.3–12.3 Write narratives to develop real or imagined experiences or events using effective technique, well-chosen details, and well-structured event sequences.				
SL.11–12.4. Present information, findings, and supporting evidence, conveying a clear and distinct perspective, such that listeners can follow the line of reasoning, alternative or opposing perspectives are addressed, and the organization, development, substance, and style are appropriate to purpose, audience, and a range of formal and informal tasks.				
Total points				

THE CHICKEN THIEF

by Beatrice Rodriguez

Lesson by Lauren M. Gay

Level	Beginning to advanced
Preparation Time	20 minutes
Length of Lesson	1 hour 10 minutes
Objective	Students will create an original dialogue to capture the interactions between the characters throughout the story.

Materials

- *The Chicken Thief* by Béatrice Rodriguez (Brooklyn, NY: Enchanted Lion Books, 2009)
- Computer
- Paper and pencils

Vocabulary

- anger
- beach
- bear
- burrow
- chase
- chicken
- fire
- footprint
- forest

- fox
- friendship
- hen
- ocean
- rabbit
- thief

Procedure

1. Conduct a picture walk of the story, stopping at each page to allow students an opportunity to see the interactions between the characters.
2. Inform students they will be working in groups to create the dialogue they believe is occurring between the characters throughout the story. Break the class into small groups of about five students for this collaborative activity. Within the group, the students will decide which character's role each will take on.
3. Have students collaboratively write the dialogue they believe is being exchanged among the characters on each page of the text. This activity can be scaffolded by providing beginning ELs the option of writing key words and ideas from the character dialogue while encouraging more advanced ELs to write more detailed dialogue.
4. Have each student group practice the lines of their script.
5. Finally, have the students in each group use video editing software, which will contain images of each page from the story, to record their script, voicing over the images.

Assessment

The teacher will review students' written scripts about the interactions in the story and their recorded speaking.

Additional Resources

Related Websites

Béatrice Rodriguez's site with reviews about the sequels to *The Chicken Thief* (can be used for follow-up discussions about why students chose the dialogue they did)—www.beatricerodriguez.com/?p=2.

Information about the red fox. Students can then discuss how the characteristics of a fox played into the story events—http://animals.nationalgeographic .com/animals/mammals/red-fox/.

Related Apps

- QuickVoice (free)—record your voice on an iPad.
- Little Story Maker (free)—add text to imported photos for story creations on an iPad.

Further Reading

Brouillette, L. (2012). Advancing the speaking and listening skills of K–2 English language learners through creative drama. *TESOL Journal, 3*(1), 138–145.

TESOL PreK–12 English Language Proficiency Standards

Standard 1: English language learners communicate for social, intercultural, and instructional purposes within the school setting.

Standard 2: English language learners communicate information, ideas, and concepts necessary for academic success in the area of language arts.

Common Core State Standards ELA Suggested Connections

The following are the Common Core State Standards for English Language Arts that are aligned with this lesson. The rubric on the next page includes a sampling of grade levels to show how the standards get more complex at higher grade levels.

Writing: W.K.3; W.1.3; W.2.3; W.3.3; W.4.3; W.5.3; W.6.3; W.7.3; W.8.3; W.9–10.3; W.11–12.3

Speaking and Listening: SL.K.4; SL.1.4; SL.2.4; SL.3.4; SL.4.4; SL.5.4; SL.6.4; SL.7.4; SL.8.4; SL.9–10.4; SL.11–12.4

THE CHICKEN THIEF

CCSS Sample Rubric

Go to www.tesol.org/wordless to complete the rubric by adding your grade level standards from the Common Core website.

Writing: http://www.corestandards.org/ELA-Literacy/W/introduction/

Speaking and Listening: http://www.corestandards.org/ELA-Literacy/SL/introduction/

	Grading Criteria			
	Outstanding 10	**Adequate 8–9**	**Developing 1–7**	**Not Present 0**
	All of the criteria are present and fully developed.	Most of the criteria are present and adequately developed.	Some of the criteria are present and somewhat developed.	None of the criteria are present.
Standards	**Teacher's Comments**			
W.K.3. Use a combination of drawing, dictating, and writing to narrate a single event or several loosely linked events, tell about the events in the order in which they occurred, and provide a reaction to what happened.				
SL.K.4. Describe familiar people, places, things, and events and, with prompting and support, provide additional detail. *or*				
W.6.3. Write narratives to develop real or imagined experiences or events using effective technique, relevant descriptive details, and well-structured event sequences.				

(continued)	Grading Criteria			
	Outstanding 10	**Adequate 8–9**	**Developing 1–7**	**Not Present 0**
	All of the criteria are present and fully developed.	Most of the criteria are present and adequately developed.	Some of the criteria are present and somewhat developed.	None of the criteria are present.
Standards	**Teacher's Comments**			
SL.6.4. Present claims and findings, sequencing ideas logically and using pertinent descriptions, facts, and details to accentuate main ideas or themes; use appropriate eye contact, adequate volume, and clear pronunciation. *or*				
W.11–12.3.Write narratives to develop real or imagined experiences or events using effective technique, well-chosen details, and well-structured event sequences.				
SL.11–12.4. Present information, findings, and supporting evidence, conveying a clear and distinct perspective, such that listeners can follow the line of reasoning, alternative or opposing perspectives are addressed, and the organization, development, substance, and style are appropriate to purpose, audience, and a range of formal and informal tasks.				
Total points				

FLORA AND THE FLAMINGO

by Molly Idle

Lesson by Jocelyn N. Anthony-Williams

Level	Beginning to advanced
Preparation Time	5–10 minutes
Length of Lesson	40–50 minutes
Objective	Students will write the story and create a video close-up of the book while narrating it.

Materials

- *Flora and the Flamingo* by Molly Idle (San Francisco, CA: Chronicle Books, 2013)
- Realistic and illustrated pictures of a flamingo
- Pictures of ballerinas and other dancers
- Markers
- Sentence strips
- Video camera
- Computer

Vocabulary

- copy
- dance
- dancer
- feet
- flamingo
- girl

- music
- pink
- play
- toes

Procedure

1. Conduct a quick introduction to the book. Introduce the words "flamingo" and "dancer." Have the class repeat the words with you.

2. Hold up flash cards showing flamingos and dancers. As you show the cards, have students repeat the word that corresponds with each picture (flamingo or dancer).

3. Place students in groups, including a mix of beginner, intermediate, and advanced readers in each group if possible.

4. Have students rotate in groups among three stations (spending 2 to 3 minutes per station). The stations consist of (1) looking at the pictures, (2) watching a video of the book online at www.youtube.com/watch?v=9d311srs7tc, and (3) reviewing the actual book.

5. Have students work in groups and write a narration for the story as though they were announcers narrating a dance competition. Students should write one to two sentences per page. Beginning students contribute to the story by adding all the details they can orally. Intermediate students write down as many words as they can. Advanced students work as editors to finalize all sentences. This work would become the script for the book.

6. Have the groups record themselves with video cameras, flipping through the pages and narrating the story as if it were a dance competition, using the online video as a model. Each student gets a speaking part.

7. As an extension activity, have students edit the video using video editing software and adding music.

Assessment

The students' written stories and their speaking skills while narrating the video are reviewed by the teacher.

Additional Resources

Related Websites

Collection of videos on dancing animals with more information and conversations about dancing animals—http://theweek.com/article/index/243068/6-animals-that-science-has-discovered-can-dance#axzz34Tad9Xdt.

Videos of other animals dancing, with judges' follow-up opinions on each activity—www.discoverwildlife.com/animals/strictly-animals-dancing.

Related Apps

- ABCmouse.com Zoo set 2 (free)—learn interesting facts about flamingos.
- One World Dictionary (free)—learn how to properly conjugate verbs.

Further Reading

Harvey, S., & Goudvis, A. (2007). *Strategies that work: Teaching comprehension* (2nd ed.). Portland, ME: Stenhouse.

TESOL PreK–12 English Language Proficiency Standards

Standard 1: English language learners communicate for social, intercultural, and instructional purposes within the school setting.

Standard 2: English language learners communicate information, ideas, and concepts necessary for academic success in the area of language arts.

Common Core State Standards ELA Suggested Connections

The following are the Common Core State Standards for English Language Arts that are aligned with this lesson. The rubric on the next page includes a sampling of grade levels to show how the standards get more complex at higher grade levels.

Writing: W.K.3; W.1.3; W.2.3; W.3.3; W.4.3; W.5.3; W.6.3; W.7.3; W.8.3; W.9–10.3; W.11–12.3

Speaking and Listening: SL.K.4; SL.1.4; SL.2.4; SL.3.4; SL.4.4; SL.5.4; SL.6.4; SL.7.4; SL.8.4; SL.9–10.4; SL.11–12.4

FLORA AND THE FLAMINGO

CCSS Sample Rubric

Go to www.tesol.org/wordless to complete the rubric by adding your grade level standards from the Common Core website.

Writing: http://www.corestandards.org/ELA-Literacy/W/introduction/

Speaking and Listening: http://www.corestandards.org/ELA-Literacy/SL/introduction/

	Grading Criteria			
	Outstanding 10	Adequate 8–9	Developing 1–7	Not Present 0
	All of the criteria are present and fully developed.	Most of the criteria are present and adequately developed.	Some of the criteria are present and somewhat developed.	None of the criteria are present.
Standards	Teacher's Comments			
W.K.3. Use a combination of drawing, dictating, and writing to narrate a single event or several loosely linked events, tell about the events in the order in which they occurred, and provide a reaction to what happened.				
SL.K.4. Describe familiar people, places, things, and events and, with prompting and support, provide additional detail.				
SL.6.4. Present claims and findings, sequencing ideas logically and using pertinent descriptions, facts, and details to accentuate main ideas or themes; use appropriate eye contact, adequate volume, and clear pronunciation. *or*				

(continued)	Grading Criteria			
	Outstanding 10	**Adequate 8–9**	**Developing 1–7**	**Not Present 0**
	All of the criteria are present and fully developed.	Most of the criteria are present and adequately developed.	Some of the criteria are present and somewhat developed.	None of the criteria are present.
Standards	**Teacher's Comments**			
W.6.3–12.3. Write narratives to develop real or imagined experiences or events using effective technique, relevant descriptive details/ well-chosen details, and well-structured event sequences.				
SL.11–12.4. Present information, findings, and supporting evidence, conveying a clear and distinct perspective, such that listeners can follow the line of reasoning, alternative or opposing perspectives are addressed, and the organization, development, substance, and style are appropriate to purpose, audience, and a range of formal and informal tasks.				
Total points				

THE LION AND THE MOUSE

by Jerry Pinkney

Lesson by Jocelyn N. Anthony-Williams

Level	Beginning to advanced
Preparation Time	15 minutes
Length of Lesson	40–50 minutes
Objective	Students will complete a cloze activity using words in the correct context.

Materials

- *The Lion and the Mouse* by Jerry Pinkney (New York, NY: Little, Brown and Company, 2009)
- Word cards with pictures
- Word cards without pictures
- Sentence starter strips
- Cloze reading papers

Vocabulary

- afraid
- catch
- friend
- happy
- help
- lion
- mouse
- need
- net
- tie

Procedure

1. Show students picture cards (with no words) from the story. Encourage students to describe what they are seeing in the pictures. (The pictures do not have to be in order.)

2. After showing the class all the pictures, ask students to predict what will happen in the story.

3. Go through the book the first time, only showing pictures and asking students to explain what they see.

4. Go through the book a second time, page by page, showing the students picture cards with words on them. For example, show the students a picture of the mouse shaking that corresponds with the page, and say, "The mouse is afraid. What does 'afraid' mean? Or, "The lion is happy. What does the word 'happy' mean? Can you show me 'happy'"? Have students act out happy.

5. Have students take turns acting out the descriptive words (adjectives).

6. Then have students work independently, filling in cloze sentence strips to tell what happened. (Cloze sentences have words blanked out.) Beginning students should only have one word to fill in for a very short summary. Intermediate students can have a slightly longer summary to fill in that has more blank words. Advanced students can have the longest passage to fill in.

7. Next, have groups of two or three students read their summaries to each other.

8. Finally, give students time to retell what they believe happened, making sure they use the word cards with pictures to help them narrate.

Assessment

Students' writing on the cloze assignment will be reviewed to check if they understood and used the words in the correct context.

Additional Resources

Related Websites

Aesop's fables for children for follow-up discussions—www.read.gov/aesop /007.html.

A podcast of the story students could listen to while viewing the story— www.childclassics.com/.

A retelling of the story students could use to check their predictions against the actual story—http://pbskids.org/lions/stories/.

Related Apps

- ABCMouse.com (free)—introduce students to zoo animals and their sounds. Students learn interesting facts about animals and can take interactive quizzes as they learn new information about specific animals. Available on iTunes and Google play.
- Real Animals HD ($2.99)—see 3-D, lifelike animals in their habitats. Available on iTunes and Google play.

Further Reading

Albasha, R. (2014). *Grammar and adjectives.* Retrieved from: http://www.tesol .org/connect/tesol-resource-center/search-details/lesson-plans/2014/05/15 /grammar-and-adjectives.

TESOL PreK–12 English Language Proficiency Standards

Standard 1: English language learners communicate for social, intercultural, and instructional purposes within the school setting.

Standard 2: English language learners communicate information, ideas, and concepts necessary for academic success in the area of language arts.

Common Core State Standards ELA Suggested Connections

The following are the Common Core State Standards for English Language Arts that are aligned with this lesson. The rubric on the next page includes a sampling of grade levels to show how the standards get more complex at higher grade levels.

Writing: W.K.3; W.1.3; W.2.3; W.3.3; W.4.3; W.5.3; W.6.3; W.7.3; W.8.3; W.9–10.3; W.11–12.3

THE LION AND THE MOUSE

CCSS Sample Rubric

Go to www.tesol.org/wordless to complete the rubric by adding your grade level standards from the Common Core website.

Writing: http://www.corestandards.org/ELA-Literacy/W/introduction/

	Grading Criteria			
	Outstanding 10	**Adequate 8–9**	**Developing 1–7**	**Not Present 0**
	All of the criteria are present and fully developed.	Most of the criteria are present and adequately developed.	Some of the criteria are present and somewhat developed.	None of the criteria are present.
Standards	**Teacher's Comments**			
W.K.3. Use a combination of drawing, dictating, and writing to narrate a single event or several loosely linked events, tell about the events in the order in which they occurred, and provide a reaction to what happened. *or*				
W.6.3–12.3. Write narratives to develop real or imagined experiences or events using effective technique, relevant descriptive details/ well-chosen details, and well-structured event sequences.				
Total points				

THE SNOWMAN

by Raymond Briggs

Lesson by Lauren M. Gay

Level	Beginning to advanced
Preparation Time	5 minutes
Length of Lesson	50 minutes
Objective	Students will use an original "snow creature" sculpture as inspiration to compose a narrative writing piece which incorporates newly acquired vocabulary.

Materials

- *The Snowman* by Raymond Briggs (New York, NY: Random House Children's Books, 1978)
- Modeling clay
- Paper and pencils
- Computer and digital scrapbooking and photo collage software such as Little Story Maker, Story Creator, or Pixie

Vocabulary

- balloon
- fire
- flashlight
- flying
- freezer
- heat
- light

- melt
- snowman
- steam
- sunrise

Procedure

1. Do a picture walk of the story, pausing only for a moment on each page to provide the students an opportunity to gain an understanding of the story's plot.

2. Pass out modeling clay to each student. Instruct the students to create their very own "snow creature."

3. Once the students have constructed their snow creature, have them jot down ideas for a creative narrative about an adventure that they go on with their snow creature.

4. Let students use the ideas inspired by the creation of their snow creature to brainstorm and write a creative narrative. To scaffold the activity for beginning ELs, have students draw the scenes of their narrative story and label the activities that they and their snow creature do during their adventure. More advanced ELs could write a detailed description of their adventure that corresponds with their illustrations.

5. Finally, let students use a software app that allows for the integration of illustrations and text, such as Little Story Maker, Story Creator, or Pixie, to publish a final copy of their creative narratives.

Assessment

The students' written creative narrative will be reviewed by the teacher.

Additional Resources

Related Websites

Sculptures from the U.S. National Snow Sculpting Competition, which could be used to provoke student thinking or for follow-up discussion— www.usnationals.org/.

Sculptures for the McCall Area Chamber of Commerce Winter Carnival— http://mccallchamber.org/index.php?mact=Album,mff022,default,1 &mff022albumid=8&mff022returnid=107&page=107.

Related Apps

- Snowman (free)—create Snowmen on an iPad.
- Story Creator Pro (free)—create photo books of sculptures and story illustrations with text on an iPad.

Further Reading

Laman, T. T. (2013). *From idea to words: Writing strategies for the English language learners.* Portsmouth, NH: Heinemann.

TESOL PreK–12 English Language Proficiency Standards

Standard 1: English language learners communicate for social, intercultural, and instructional purposes within the school setting.

Standard 2: English language learners communicate information, ideas, and concepts necessary for academic success in the area of language arts.

Common Core State Standards ELA Suggested Connections

The following are the Common Core State Standards for English Language Arts that are aligned with this lesson. The rubric on the next page includes a sampling of grade levels to show how the standards get more complex at higher grade levels.

Writing: W.K.3; W.1.3; W.2.3; W.3.3; W.4.3; W.5.3; W.6.3; W.7.3; W.8.3; W.9–10.3; W.11–12.3

THE SNOWMAN

CCSS Sample Rubric

Go to www.tesol.org/wordless to complete the rubric by adding your grade level standards from the Common Core website.

Writing: http://www.corestandards.org/ELA-Literacy/W/introduction/

Standards	Grading Criteria			
	Outstanding 10	**Adequate 8–9**	**Developing 1–7**	**Not Present 0**
	All of the criteria are present and fully developed.	Most of the criteria are present and adequately developed.	Some of the criteria are present and somewhat developed.	None of the criteria are present.
Standards	**Teacher's Comments**			
W.K.3. Use a combination of drawing, dictating, and writing to narrate a single event or several loosely linked events, tell about the events in the order in which they occurred, and provide a reaction to what happened. *or*				
W.6.3–12.3. Write narratives to develop real or imagined experiences or events using effective technique, relevant descriptive details/ well-chosen details, and well-structured event sequences.				
Total points				

STORIES WITH MORE COMPLICATED PICTURES TO FOLLOW

SIDEWALK CIRCUS

by Paul Fleishman and Kevin Hawkes

Lesson by Jessica Karbassi

Level	Beginning to intermediate
Preparation Time	10 minutes
Length of Lesson	50 minutes
Objective	Students will participate in collaborative conversations with partners or in small groups to create circus acts.

Materials

- *Sidewalk Circus* by Paul Fleishman and Kevin Hawkes (Somerville, MA: Candlewick Press, 2004)
- Video camera
- Computer
- Top hat and other classroom materials that can be used as circus props

Vocabulary

- excited
- imagination
- juggling
- stilts
- tightrope
- trapeze
- wonder

Procedure

1. Show students video clips of real circus acts and ringmasters.

2. Do a picture walk and have students discuss what is happening on each page and how it relates to the circus.

3. Put students in groups of three and assign each group two pages from the story to re-create using classroom materials. Students can alternate within the group who will be the ringmaster that announces each act. For example, if a group is assigned the juggling pages, one student would be the ringmaster announcing what will happen, and the other two students would simulate juggling using classroom materials.

4. Give students time to brainstorm with their groups and gather the necessary materials to perform their circus act. Circulate through the classroom and check with each group to facilitate discussion.

5. Once the students have had enough time to brainstorm, record each group performing their circus act. The "ringmaster" will articulate what the group is doing.

6. Last, using video editing software, create a polished movie titled *Classroom Circus* incorporating each group's circus act.

Assessment

The students' speaking and listening skills can be observed while the groups are brainstorming and performing their circus acts.

Additional Resources

Related Websites

Video that talks about a day in life of the circus (including a discussion with a ringmaster), which students could view prior to reading Sidewalk Circus— www.youtube.com/watch?v=JyLtMTNxjK8.

Video of kindergarteners putting on a circus day. Students could view this video to get ideas on how to put together their own circus acts—www.youtube .com/watch?v=TT8mixxslVk.

Related Apps

- ABC Circus (free or $3.99)—reinforces letter and number recognition using a circus theme. Available on iTunes and Google play.
- Animal Circus Math (free)—reinforces counting, adding, subtracting, and so forth, using a circus theme. Available on iTunes.

Further Reading

For additional resources and articles about teaching EL students speaking and listening strategies, visit www.scholastic.com/teachers/article/teaching -ell-speaking-strategies.

TESOL PreK–12 English Language Proficiency Standards

Standard 1: English language learners communicate for social, intercultural, and instructional purposes within the school setting.

Standard 2: English language learners communicate information, ideas, and concepts necessary for academic success in the area of language arts.

Common Core State Standards ELA Suggested Connections

The following are the Common Core State Standards for English Language Arts that are aligned with this lesson. The rubric on the next page includes a sampling of grade levels to show how the standards get more complex at higher grade levels.

Speaking and Listening: SL.K.1; SL.1.1; SL.2.1; SL.3.1; SL.4.1

SIDEWALK CIRCUS

CCSS Sample Rubric

Go to www.tesol.org/wordless to complete the rubric by adding your grade level standards from the Common Core website.

Speaking and Listening: http://www.corestandards.org/ELA-Literacy/SL /introduction/

	Grading Criteria			
	Outstanding 10	**Adequate 8–9**	**Developing 1–7**	**Not Present 0**
	All of the criteria are present and fully developed.	Most of the criteria are present and adequately developed.	Some of the criteria are present and somewhat developed.	None of the criteria are present.
Standards	**Teacher's Comments**			
SL.K.1. Participate in collaborative conversations with diverse partners about *kindergarten topics and texts* with peers and adults in small and larger groups. *or*				
SL.4.1. Engage effectively in a range of collaborative discussions (one-on-one, in groups, and teacher-led) with diverse partners on *grade 4 topics and texts,* building on others' ideas and expressing their own clearly.				
Total points				

JOURNEY

by Aaron Becker

Lesson by Rachel H. Mrozek

Level	Intermediate to advanced
Preparation Time	10 minutes
Length of Lesson	1 hour 15 minutes
Objective	The students will write narratives into comic strip software or templates and record themselves using audio recording software.

Materials

- *Journey* by Aaron Becker (Somerville, MA: Candlewick Press, 2013)
- Computer
- Comic strip software, templates, or website, such as Comic Life
- Audio recording software, such as Garageband

Vocabulary

- castle
- crayon
- culture
- curiosity
- fantasy
- friendship
- hot air balloon
- imagination
- journey
- magic

Procedure

1. Show a short book trailer of *Journey* using Aaron Becker's website. Doing so will allow students to make text-to-self connections and relate more to the content and story of the book.

2. Next, "read" the book aloud to students. During this time, students would have a sequencing page or comic strip template to write down what they believe is happening in the story, while you slowly go through the pages. For beginnings ELs, provide a beginning, middle, and end comic strip or sequence template, and as students become more advanced more panels could be added to provide more specific details. Additionally, beginning ELs could write a one-word caption on their templates. More advanced ELs can be expected to write a few sentences to summarize the panels as well as discuss mood and tone.

3. Have students discuss their summaries in small groups. Facilitate the discussions, allowing students to point out differences they noticed, how they interpreted details, and so forth. This will segue into the next part of the lesson.

4. After the students have discussed their summaries, have students write a personal narrative as if they were the girl in the story going on their own journey. Show how students' summaries may be different because their imaginations and experiences are different, and point out that this will become more apparent as students write their own journey.

5. To further prepare students for writing, share the short documentary on the making of *Journey*, from Aaron Becker's website, to inspire the students to tap into their imaginations when they write their personal narratives.

6. Have students use comic strip software to write a comic strip of their journey.

7. Finally, when students have finished their comic strip narrative, have them record themselves reading their story using audio recording software. Compile their recordings to make a class CD to send home, and make a class book of the personal narratives.

Assessment

The students' written comic strips and their speaking on the recordings of their journey will be reviewed.

Additional Resources

Related Websites

Author Aaron Becker's website, which the teacher could use for prereading and prewriting support—www.storybreathing.com/.

CultureGrams Kids, which has videos, pictures, interviews, and so forth, of places around the world, which could be used to help students build background knowledge about journeys and places that are used in the girl's imagination in the story. The teacher could use this for prereading support—http://online.culturegrams.com/kids/index.php.

Related Apps

- Wonderopolis (free)—offers a "wonder of the day" that asks an interesting question, inquiring about places, events, and so forth. Available on iTunes and Google play.
- FaceTalker (free)—upload an image, which will "speak," mimicking the student's mouth as the voice plays back a recording; can be used instead of GarageBand. Available on iTunes.

Further Reading

Robertson, K. (2008). *Preparing ELLs to be 21st-century learners*. Retrieved from http://www.colorincolorado.org/article/21431/.

TESOL PreK–12 English Language Proficiency Standards

Standard 1: English language learners communicate for social, intercultural, and instructional purposes within the school setting.

Standard 2: English language learners communicate information, ideas, and concepts necessary for academic success in the area of language arts.

Common Core State Standards ELA Suggested Connections

The following are the Common Core State Standards for English Language Arts that are aligned with this lesson. The rubric on the next page includes a sampling of grade levels to show how the standards get more complex at higher grade levels.

Writing: W.3.3; W.4.3; W.5.3; W.6.3; W.7.3; W.8.3; W.9–10.3; W.11–12.3

Speaking and Listening: SL.3.4; SL.4.4; SL.5.4; SL.6.4; SL.7.4; SL.8.4; SL.9–10.4; SL.11–12.4

JOURNEY

CCSS Sample Rubric

Go to www.tesol.org/wordless to complete the rubric by adding your grade level standards from the Common Core website.

Writing: http://www.corestandards.org/ELA-Literacy/W/introduction/

Speaking and Listening: http://www.corestandards.org/ELA-Literacy/SL /introduction/

	Grading Criteria			
	Outstanding 10	**Adequate 8–9**	**Developing 1–7**	**Not Present 0**
	All of the criteria are present and fully developed.	Most of the criteria are present and adequately developed.	Some of the criteria are present and somewhat developed.	None of the criteria are present.
Standards	**Teacher's Comments**			
W.3.3. Write narratives to develop real or imagined experiences or events using effective technique, descriptive details, and clear event sequences.				
SL.3.4. Report on a topic or text, tell a story, or recount an experience with appropriate facts and relevant, descriptive details, speaking clearly at an understandable pace.				
SL.6.4. Present claims and findings, sequencing ideas logically and using pertinent descriptions, facts, and details to accentuate main ideas or themes; use appropriate eye contact, adequate volume, and clear pronunciation. *or*				

(continued)	Grading Criteria			
	Outstanding 10	**Adequate 8–9**	**Developing 1–7**	**Not Present 0**
	All of the criteria are present and fully developed.	Most of the criteria are present and adequately developed.	Some of the criteria are present and somewhat developed.	None of the criteria are present.
Standards	**Teacher's Comments**			
W.6.3–12.3. Write narratives to develop real or imagined experiences or events using effective technique, relevant descriptive details/ well-chosen details, and well-structured event sequences.				
SL.11–12.4. Present information, findings, and supporting evidence, conveying a clear and distinct perspective, such that listeners can follow the line of reasoning, alternative or opposing perspectives are addressed, and the organization, development, substance, and style are appropriate to purpose, audience, and a range of formal and informal tasks.				
Total points				

MIRROR

by Jeannie Baker

Lesson by Rachel H. Mrozek

Level	Intermediate to advanced
Preparation Time	20 minutes
Length of Lesson	45 minutes
Objective	The students will discuss their family routines after completing Venn diagrams to organize their thoughts. Then, they will complete and present a collage they create. Their presentation will be videotaped.

Materials

- *Mirror* by Jeannie Baker (Somerville, MA: Candlewick Press, 2010)
- Computer
- Kidspiration (http://www.inspiration.com/Kidspiration) or Venn diagram paper template
- Movie editing software such as iMovie or Windows Movie Maker
- Video camera
- Construction paper
- Markers
- Newspaper or other scraps of paper
- Various art supplies for creating a collage

Vocabulary

- Australia
- culture

- family
- meals
- mirror
- Morocco
- perspective
- routine
- rural
- urban

Procedure

1. Explore Australia and Morocco on Google Earth with the class.
2. Go through the book fairly quickly so students can discover its main idea.
3. Go through the picture book more slowly. This time, give students a Venn diagram, either a paper version or one using Kidspiration. Have students take notes during reading to show how the students' days in the book are alike and different. Beginning ELs can draw pictures to represent their comparisons, while more advanced students can write in-depth comparisons.
4. After reading, divide students into groups of two. Give them a specific topic related to events in the story, such as morning routine, dinner, errands, and so forth. They will discuss with their partner how this routine looks in their family. Their discussions can then focus on how the routines are similar and different.
5. When students are finished discussing, give them construction paper, markers, newspaper, glue, and other art materials. Have them each make a collage with a caption to represent their family's routine on the topic given for a class-book version of *Mirror*.
6. Video the pairs presenting their collages. Have them stand near each other (holding a mirror between them, their collages held up in their other hand) and have them read their captions aloud. Use video editing software to create a class video of their collages.
7. Collect the students' collages in a class book.

Assessment

The students' Venn diagrams, collages, and videos will be reviewed.

Additional Resources

Related Websites

For book preview the students could explore Australia and Morocco on Google Earth—www.google.com/earth/.

As a follow-up, students could research a country to find its similarities and differences to theirs using any of the following websites—

- http://kids.nationalgeographic.com/#
- http://worldbookonline.com/training/student/
- www.pebblego.com.

Related Apps

- Little Story Creator (free)—create digital collages and scrapbooks on iPhone and iPad.
- Kids Planet Discovery (free)—play games, watch videos, and so forth, to learn about the world's geography, nature, and cultures on an iPhone and iPad.

Further Reading

Guccione, L. (2012). *Oral language development and ELLs: 5 challenges and solutions.* Retrieved from http://www.colorincolorado.org/article/50910/.

TESOL PreK–12 English Language Proficiency Standards

Standard 1: English language learners communicate for social, intercultural, and instructional purposes within the school setting.

Standard 2: English language learners communicate information, ideas, and concepts necessary for academic success in the area of language arts.

Common Core State Standards ELA Suggested Connections

The following are the Common Core State Standards for English Language Arts that are aligned with this lesson. The rubric on the next page includes a sampling of grade levels to show how the standards get more complex at higher grade levels.

Writing: W.3.3; W.4.3; W.5.3; W.6.3; W.7.3; W.8.3; W.9–10.3; W.11–12.3

Speaking and Listening: SL.3.4; SL.4.4; SL.5.4; SL.6.4; SL.7.4; SL.8.4; SL.9–10.4; SL.11–12.4

MIRROR

CCSS Sample Rubric

Go to www.tesol.org/wordless to complete the rubric by adding your grade level standards from the Common Core website.

Writing: http://www.corestandards.org/ELA-Literacy/W/introduction/

Speaking and Listening: http://www.corestandards.org/ELA-Literacy/SL/introduction/

	Grading Criteria			
	Outstanding 10	**Adequate 8–9**	**Developing 1–7**	**Not Present 0**
	All of the criteria are present and fully developed.	Most of the criteria are present and adequately developed.	Some of the criteria are present and somewhat developed.	None of the criteria are present.
Standards	**Teacher's Comments**			
W.3.3. Write narratives to develop real or imagined experiences or events using effective technique, descriptive details, and clear event sequences.				
SL.3.4. Report on a topic or text, tell a story, or recount an experience with appropriate facts and relevant, descriptive details, speaking clearly at an understandable pace. *or*				
W.6.3–12.3. Write narratives to develop real or imagined experiences or events using effective technique, relevant descriptive details/ well-chosen details, and well-structured event sequences.				

(continued)

	Grading Criteria			
	Outstanding 10	**Adequate 8–9**	**Developing 1–7**	**Not Present 0**
	All of the criteria are present and fully developed.	Most of the criteria are present and adequately developed.	Some of the criteria are present and somewhat developed.	None of the criteria are present.
Standards	**Teacher's Comments**			
SL.6.4. Present claims and findings, sequencing ideas logically and using pertinent descriptions, facts, and details to accentuate main ideas or themes; use appropriate eye contact, adequate volume, and clear pronunciation. *or*				
SL.11–12.4. Present information, findings, and supporting evidence, conveying a clear and distinct perspective, such that listeners can follow the line of reasoning, alternative or opposing perspectives are addressed, and the organization, development, substance, and style are appropriate to purpose, audience, and a range of formal and informal tasks.				
Total points				

FLOTSAM

by David Wiesner

Lesson by Judith Cruzado-Guerrero

Level	Beginning to advanced
Preparation Time	5 minutes
Length of Lesson	45 minutes
Objective	The students will discuss an illustration from the book with their partner while providing details.

Materials

- *Flotsam* by David Wiesner (New York, NY: Clarion Books, 1991)
- Mystery bag with items related to the book (camera, film, magnifying glass, shells, sand, etc.)
- Copy of illustrations from book (e.g., underwater shots, people)

Vocabulary

- beach
- camera
- fish
- flotsam
- magnifying glass
- ocean
- octopus
- sea shells
- starfish
- turtles

Procedure

Before reading

1. Share a mystery bag with items related to the book (sand, shells, camera, film, photos, etc.). As the items are shared with the class, ask questions to activate prior knowledge and connect to prior experiences. Focus the discussion on the beach and objects washed up by the sea.

   a. Beach photo—Have you been to the beach? What kind of things do you see at the beach?

   b. Sand, shells—What do you do at the beach? Have you found objects at the beach? Where do you think they come from?

   c. Camera—What do you do with a camera? What kind of camera is this one? Why would you use a camera at the beach? If you found a camera, what kind of photos would you want to take? Why?

2. Introduce the book by showing the cover and reading the title. Ask students what "flotsam" means. After listening to the students' responses, provide a student friendly definition. Then ask students what they think the book is about after examining the cover and items in the mystery bag. Have them write their predictions.

During reading

3. Go through the entire book, and ask students to pay attention to the details on each page. Ask questions throughout the story: What do you see on this page? Do you think the illustration is real or make-believe? Why?

After reading

4. Allow students to work with a partner. Give each student pair a copy of an illustration from the book and/or an item from the mystery bag (e.g., underwater shots). Have students discuss the image with their partner, describing what is happening in the image using details from the illustrations. This will give students the opportunity to use their imagination, express their ideas, and listen to their partner. Beginning ELs could share vocabulary words to identify or describe the illustration, whereas more advanced ELs could add details about what is happening in the illustration. The focus of the speaking task would vary depending on the English proficiency levels and needs of the students. The students will need to agree about what they will report back to the class.

5. To reduce students' anxiety about speaking in class, audio record the students rather than have them share to the whole group. The recordings could be added to the listening center.

Assessment

The students' spoken responses will be assessed by the teacher during their presentations.

Additional Resources

Related Websites

David Wiesner's website, where students could see other books he has written
and conduct an author study and make text-to-text connections—
www.hmhbooks.com/wiesner/index.html.

A student interview of David Wiesner. Students could follow the format to
interview each other—www.timeforkids.com/news/qa-david-wiesner/2986.

Students could see real images of flotsam by looking up articles about tsunamis
or by searching for flotsam images online to make a content-area
connection.

Related Apps

• GeoDash ($1.99)—learn more about the environment with this National
Geographic for Kids app. Available on iTunes.
• Ocean Sounds Relax n Sleep (free)—create a soothing classroom environ-
ment. Available on Google play.

Further Reading

Online Teaching Activity Index: Audio Recording and Podcasting—http://
www.ion.uillinois.edu/resources/otai/Audio.asp.

TESOL PreK–12 English Language Proficiency Standards

Standard 1: English language learners communicate for social, intercultural,
and instructional purposes within the school setting.

Standard 2: English language learners communicate information, ideas, and
concepts necessary for academic success in the area of language arts.

Common Core State Standards ELA Suggested Connections

The following are the Common Core State Standards for English Language
Arts that are aligned with this lesson. The rubric on the next page includes a
sampling of grade levels to show how the standards get more complex at higher
grade levels.

Speaking and Listening: SL.K.4; SL.1.4; SL.2.4; SL.3.4; SL.4.4; SL.5.4; SL.6.4;
SL.7.4; SL.8.4; SL.9–10.4; SL.11–12.4

FLOTSAM

CCSS Sample Rubric

Go to www.tesol.org/wordless to complete the rubric by adding your grade level standards from the Common Core website.

Speaking and Listening: http://www.corestandards.org/ELA-Literacy/SL /introduction/

	Grading Criteria			
	Outstanding 10	**Adequate 8–9**	**Developing 1–7**	**Not Present 0**
	All of the criteria are present and fully developed.	Most of the criteria are present and adequately developed.	Some of the criteria are present and somewhat developed.	None of the criteria are present.
Standards	**Teacher's Comments**			
SL.K.4. Describe familiar people, places, things, and events and, with prompting and support, provide additional detail. *or*				
SL.6.4. Present claims and findings, sequencing ideas logically and using pertinent descriptions, facts, and details to accentuate main ideas or themes; use appropriate eye contact, adequate volume, and clear pronunciation. *or*				

(continued)

	Grading Criteria			
	Outstanding 10	**Adequate 8–9**	**Developing 1–7**	**Not Present 0**
	All of the criteria are present and fully developed.	Most of the criteria are present and adequately developed.	Some of the criteria are present and somewhat developed.	None of the criteria are present.
Standards	**Teacher's Comments**			
SL.11–12.4. Present information, findings, and supporting evidence, conveying a clear and distinct perspective, such that listeners can follow the line of reasoning, alternative or opposing perspectives are addressed, and the organization, development, substance, and style are appropriate to purpose, audience, and a range of formal and informal tasks.				
Total points				

FREE FALL

by David Wiesner

Lesson by Alyssa J. Sanderson

Level	Beginning to advanced
Preparation Time	10 minutes
Length of Lesson	Two sessions, 50 minutes each
Objective	Students will record the dialogue they create for their story and use video editing software to edit their recordings.

Materials

- *Free Fall* by David Wiesner (New York, NY: Harper Collins, 1988), one copy per group of two to three students
- Sticky notes
- Paper and pencils
- Writing journal (one per student)
- Computer with video editing software such as iMovie

Vocabulary

- asleep
- castle
- chess
- dream
- field
- forest
- quilt
- shield

Procedure

1. Explain to students that they are going to focus on questioning while reading as a way to understand a wordless picture book. Model how to ask questions to gain understanding in the first several pages of the story, allowing students to intervene when necessary. Write down your questions on sticky notes and put them on the pages in the book that they apply to. Questions can include but are not limited to the following: What time of day is it? Where are they in the world? What time period is it? How do the characters know one another? Why do you think that? How do you know? What would you do if . . . ? I wonder why . . . ? Allow students to state their opinions to the questions as they are presented while reading. About halfway through the story, give each student one sticky note and ask him or her to think of a question while reading the rest of the book and write it down. As they write down their questions, have students come up, read their question (if they feel comfortable enough), and stick their question on the page in your book. Discuss questions as necessary. Do this until the entire book has been read and all students are given an opportunity to share their questions.

2. Place students in predetermined groups of two to three and give them a copy of the book. Together in small groups, allow students to write down dialogue for the characters from the beginning to the end of the story in their writing journals.

3. Last, have each group of students make an audio recording of their dialogue and use kid friendly editing software to edit their recordings. Students will record their voices reading their dialogue. Once that is completed, have each willing group take turns playing their recording while flipping through the book to show the class their story.

Assessment

The recordings of the dialogue will be reviewed by the teacher.

Additional Resources

Related Websites

Dream article on the PBS Kids website, where students could get a closer look at dreams and why kids dream—http://pbskids.org/itsmylife/emotions/dreams/article2.html.

Information for students about questioning as a comprehension strategy (Into the Book website)—http://reading.ecb.org/.

Related Apps

- Write about This (free)—create stories using dialogue, pictures, and personalized voice recordings on the iPad.
- Geek Kids Chess Academy Lite (free)—play chess on the iPad.

Further Reading

Lacina, J., Levine, N., Sowa, P., & Suarez, D. (Eds.). (2007). *Helping English language learners succeed in preK–elementary*. Alexandria, VA: TESOL International Association.

TESOL PreK–12 English Language Proficiency Standards

Standard 1: English language learners communicate for social, intercultural, and instructional purposes within the school setting.

Standard 2: English language learners communicate information, ideas, and concepts necessary for academic success in the area of language arts.

Common Core State Standards ELA Suggested Connections

The following are the Common Core State Standards for English Language Arts that are aligned with this lesson. The rubric on the next page includes a sampling of grade levels to show how the standards get more complex at higher grade levels.

Speaking and Listening: SL.K.4; SL.1.4; SL.2.4; SL.3.4; SL.4.4; SL.5.4; SL.6.4; SL.7.4; SL.8.4; SL.9–10.4; SL.11–12.4 and SL.K.5; SL.1.5; SL.2.5; SL.3.5; SL.4.5; SL.5.5; SL.6.5; SL.7.5; SL.8.5; SL.9–10.5; SL.11–12.5

FREE FALL

CCSS Sample Rubric

Go to www.tesol.org/wordless to complete the rubric by adding your grade level standards from the Common Core website.

Speaking and Listening: http://www.corestandards.org/ELA-Literacy/SL/introduction/

	Grading Criteria			
	Outstanding 10	**Adequate 8–9**	**Developing 1–7**	**Not Present 0**
	All of the criteria are present and fully developed.	Most of the criteria are present and adequately developed.	Some of the criteria are present and somewhat developed.	None of the criteria are present.
Standards	**Teacher's Comments**			
SL.K.4. Describe familiar people, places, things, and events and, with prompting and support, provide additional detail.				
SL.K.5. Add drawings or other visual displays to descriptions as desired to provide additional detail. *or*				
SL.6.4. Present claims and findings, sequencing ideas logically and using pertinent descriptions, facts, and details to accentuate main ideas or themes; use appropriate eye contact, adequate volume, and clear pronunciation.				

(continued)

	Grading Criteria			
	Outstanding 10	**Adequate 8–9**	**Developing 1–7**	**Not Present 0**
	All of the criteria are present and fully developed.	Most of the criteria are present and adequately developed.	Some of the criteria are present and somewhat developed.	None of the criteria are present.
Standards	**Teacher's Comments**			
SL.6.5. Include multimedia components (e.g., graphics, images, music, sound) and visual displays in presentations to clarify information. *or*				
SL.11–12.4. Present information, findings, and supporting evidence, conveying a clear and distinct perspective, such that listeners can follow the line of reasoning, alternative or opposing perspectives are addressed, and the organization, development, substance, and style are appropriate to purpose, audience, and a range of formal and informal tasks.				
SL.11–12.5. Make strategic use of digital media (e.g., textual, graphical, audio, visual, and interactive elements) in presentations to enhance understanding of findings, reasoning, and evidence and to add interest.				
Total points				

TUESDAY

by David Wiesner

Lesson by Alyssa J. Sanderson

Level	Beginning to advanced
Preparation Time	15 minutes
Length of Lesson	1 hour
Objective	In groups, students will create a sequel to the story by drawing pictures and will then figure out through discussions with their group what other groups' sequences of pictures mean.

Materials

- *Tuesday* by David Wiesner (New York, NY: Clarion Books, 1991)
- Photocopies of pages 7–8, 11–12, 15–16, 19–20, 25–26 in bags (five sets)
- Projector or document camera
- 8.5-by-11 inch paper
- Pencils, colored pencils, markers, crayons
- Compare-and-contrast Venn diagram

Vocabulary

- flew
- flying
- frogs
- grandfather clock
- investigator
- lily pads
- neighborhood

- nighttime
- pigs
- silhouette

Procedure

1. Put students into predetermined groups and pass out a bag of pictures to each group. Based on the pictures, students will work cooperatively and collaboratively to predetermine the order of events from the story (what will happen first, next, then, etc.).

2. While students are still sitting in their groups with their pictures laid out, read the story aloud, and show it on the projector so that all students can see it from where they are sitting. As you turn each page, give students a minute to discuss with their group members what is happening in the picture. While listening and discussing, students will also be checking their pictures to see if they have them in the correct order. Students can rearrange the order of their pictures as needed. Allow groups to share their ideas to the whole class to clarify the events taking place.

3. Then, have each group create a five-event sequel to the story using only hand-drawn pictures. Give students five sheets of paper (or one per group member) and ask them to draw the next five things that might happen. To get them started, ask questions such as the following: What kind of trouble will the pigs get into? Will they come to a neighborhood again? How will the pictures tell us what time of day it is? Will the pigs get caught? Have the students in the group collaborate so that they each create a picture in sequential order.

4. Once each group has completed their sequel and laid it out, have the group members rotate to another group's sequel. Each group will work together to verbally retell the events that are happening in that sequel. As an extension, allow group members to compare and contrast their group's sequel to another group's sequel using a Venn diagram.

Assessment

Students will be graded on their speaking and listening skills during their group activities, specifically when creating their own individual picture for their group's sequel.

Additional Resources

Related Websites

David Wiesner's homepage, which can be used for follow-up discussions on artistry and to see other wordless picture books by the author—www.hmhbooks.com/wiesner/.

National Geographic Kids, which has information on the American bullfrog—http://kids.nationalgeographic.com/kids/animals/creaturefeature/american-bullfrog/.

Related Apps

- Frogger (free)—play a fun frog game on an iPad.
- Interactive Telling Time Lite (free)—tell time on an iPad.

Further Reading

Bresser, R., Melanese, K., & Sphar, C. (2009). *Supporting English language learners in math class, grades K–2.* Sausalito, CA: Math Solutions Publications.

TESOL PreK–12 English Language Proficiency Standards

Standard 1: English language learners communicate for social, intercultural, and instructional purposes within the school setting.

Standard 2: English language learners communicate information, ideas, and concepts necessary for academic success in the area of language arts.

Common Core State Standards ELA Suggested Connections

The following are the Common Core State Standards for English Language Arts that are aligned with this lesson. The rubric on the next page includes a sampling of grade levels to show how the standards get more complex at higher grade levels.

Speaking and Listening: SL.K.4; SL.1.4; SL.2.4; SL.3.4; SL.4.4; SL.5.4; SL.6.4; SL.7.4; SL.8.4; SL.9–10.4; SL.11–12.4

TUESDAY

CCSS Sample Rubric

Go to www.tesol.org/wordless to complete the rubric by adding your grade level standards from the Common Core website.

Speaking and Listening: http://www.corestandards.org/ELA-Literacy/SL/introduction/

	Grading Criteria			
	Outstanding 10	**Adequate 8–9**	**Developing 1–7**	**Not Present 0**
	All of the criteria are present and fully developed.	Most of the criteria are present and adequately developed.	Some of the criteria are present and somewhat developed.	None of the criteria are present.
Standards	**Teacher's Comments**			
SL.K.4. Describe familiar people, places, things, and events and, with prompting and support, provide additional detail. *or*				
SL.6.4. Present claims and findings, sequencing ideas logically and using pertinent descriptions, facts, and details to accentuate main ideas or themes; use appropriate eye contact, adequate volume, and clear pronunciation. *or*				

(continued)	Grading Criteria			
	Outstanding 10	**Adequate 8–9**	**Developing 1–7**	**Not Present 0**
	All of the criteria are present and fully developed.	Most of the criteria are present and adequately developed.	Some of the criteria are present and somewhat developed.	None of the criteria are present.
Standards	**Teacher's Comments**			
SL.11–12.4. Present information, findings, and supporting evidence, conveying a clear and distinct perspective, such that listeners can follow the line of reasoning, alternative or opposing perspectives are addressed, and the organization, development, substance, and style are appropriate to purpose, audience, and a range of formal and informal tasks.				
Total points				

MR. WUFFLES!

by David Wiesner

Lesson by Monica E. Cortada

Level	Beginning to advanced
Preparation Time	5 minutes
Length of Lesson	Two 50 minute sessions
Objective	Students will use sticky notes to label various items in the book, create dialogue for the characters, and then write and retell the story.

Materials

- *Mr. Wuffles!* by David Wiesner (New York, NY: Clarion Books, 2013), one copy per two students
- Various colored small sticky notes
- Paper and pencils
- Document camera (or chart paper)
- Video camera
- Computer

Vocabulary

- aliens
- ant
- cat
- cracker
- eye
- ladybug

- pounce
- radiator cover
- spaceship

Procedure

1. Provide pairs of students a copy of the book and give them time to negotiate the meaning of the story using the language that will best support meaning.

2. Group students, and have one group "translate" the aliens' and ants' speech bubbles into English, covering the speech bubbles of the ants with one color sticky note and the aliens' with a different color. Have students label objects in the pictures with sticky notes that will be needed for a retelling. Note that objects such as "radiator cover" may require teacher assistance.

3. Write the story using the vocabulary and dialogue from the sticky notes. Write interactively with students, using the document camera, chart paper, or computer.

4. Last, video the book. Pan the pages of the book with different students doing the narration and saying the character parts, and use video editing software, such as Windows Movie Maker or iMovie, to edit it.

Assessment

The students' written scripts and their speaking skills while acting out the scripts will be assessed and can also be compared to a language development continuum such as the WIDA Can Do Descriptors. WIDA Can Do Descriptors by grade level clusters can be found at www.wida.us/standards/CAN_DOs/.

Additional Resources

Related Websites

Audio recording of David Wiesner talking about the book's development (TeachingBooks.net)—www.teachingbooks.net/tb.cgi?tid=36047&a=1.

Book trailer by the publisher—www.youtube.com/watch?v=-5Z5JI17u68.

Online tool to create trading cards with favorite characters on Read, Write, Think—www.readwritethink.org/parent-afterschool-resources/activities-projects/create-trading-cards-favorite-30171.html.

Related Apps

- Toondoo (free)—design cartoons for your own cartoon alien visitation stories with this free web-based app. Available at http://www.toondoo.com/.
- Sticky (free)—create notebooks, including sticky notes, for the iPad, iPhone, and Android.

Further Reading

Johnson, B. (2014). Tools for teaching: The amazing sticky note. Retrieved from http://www.edutopia.org/blog/sticky-note-teaching-tool-ben-johnson.

TESOL PreK–12 English Language Proficiency Standards

Standard 1: English language learners communicate for social, intercultural, and instructional purposes within the school setting.

Standard 2: English language learners communicate information, ideas, and concepts necessary for academic success in the area of language arts.

Common Core State Standards ELA Suggested Connections

The following are the Common Core State Standards for English Language Arts that are aligned with this lesson. The rubric on the next page includes a sampling of grade levels to show how the standards get more complex at higher grade levels.

Writing: W.K.3; W.1.3; W.2.3; W.3.3; W.4.3; W.5.3; W.6.3; W.7.3; W.8.3; W.9–10.3; W.11–12.3

Speaking and Listening: SL.K.4; SL.1.4; SL.2.4; SL.3.4; SL.4.4; SL.5.4; SL.6.4; SL.7.4; SL.8.4; SL.9–10.4; SL.11–12.4

MR. WUFFLES

CCSS Sample Rubric

Go to www.tesol.org/wordless to complete the rubric by adding your grade level standards from the Common Core website.

Writing: http://www.corestandards.org/ELA-Literacy/W/introduction/

Speaking and Listening: http://www.corestandards.org/ELA-Literacy/SL/introduction/

	Grading Criteria			
	Outstanding 10	Adequate 8–9	Developing 1–7	Not Present 0
	All of the criteria are present and fully developed.	Most of the criteria are present and adequately developed.	Some of the criteria are present and somewhat developed.	None of the criteria are present.
Standards	**Teacher's Comments**			
W.K.3. Use a combination of drawing, dictating, and writing to narrate a single event or several loosely linked events, tell about the events in the order in which they occurred, and provide a reaction to what happened.				
SL.K.4. Describe familiar people, places, things, and events and, with prompting and support, provide additional detail. *or*				
W.3.3. Write narratives to develop real or imagined experiences or events using effective technique, descriptive details, and clear event sequences.				

(continued)

Standards	Grading Criteria			
	Outstanding 10	**Adequate 8–9**	**Developing 1–7**	**Not Present 0**
	All of the criteria are present and fully developed.	Most of the criteria are present and adequately developed.	Some of the criteria are present and somewhat developed.	None of the criteria are present.
Standards	**Teacher's Comments**			
SL.6.4. Present claims and findings, sequencing ideas logically and using pertinent descriptions, facts, and details to accentuate main ideas or themes; use appropriate eye contact, adequate volume, and clear pronunciation. *or*				
W.6.3–12.3. Write narratives to develop real or imagined experiences or events using effective technique, relevant descriptive details/ well-chosen details, and well-structured event sequences.				
SL.11–12.4. Present information, findings, and supporting evidence, conveying a clear and distinct perspective, such that listeners can follow the line of reasoning, alternative or opposing perspectives are addressed, and the organization, development, substance, and style are appropriate to purpose, audience, and a range of formal and informal tasks.				
Total points				

THE RED BOOK

by Barbara Lehman

Lesson by Malerie E. Rubnitz

Level	Beginning to advanced
Preparation Time	5 minutes
Length of Lesson	45 minutes
Objective	The students will write inferences, create stories with a new ending, and present their completed work.

Materials

- *The Red Book* by Barbara Lehman (Boston, MA: Houghton Mifflin, 2004)
- Chart paper
- Markers
- Mobile laptops (if possible)
- Pixie (www.tech4learning.com/pixie) or Kidspiration (www.inspiration.com/Kidspiration)

Vocabulary

- discover
- experience
- imagination
- magical
- snowdrift
- spies
- transported

Procedure

1. Take a picture walk and introduce the term "inference." Have the word written on chart paper and briefly discuss what it means (evidence + prior knowledge = inference).

2. Read the first three pages of the book, and model thinking aloud by using the pictures to make inferences about the story. Then, chart your thinking. Continue to model your thinking while charting your inferences on select pages throughout the beginning and middle of the book. When needed, clarify for the students any misunderstandings throughout the book.

3. Pair up the students, and have them write their inferences for the remainder of the book. Once students have completed their writing, they can volunteer to share their inferences with the class. Chart the inferences shared by the students to display in the classroom as a reference.

4. Have students work with the same partner to illustrate or write at least two events that happen next in the story, based on the inferences they made as they read the book. The students can choose to use Pixie or Kidspiration software to complete their new story. If time allows, students can share their new story with the class.

Assessment

The students' written inferences, story creations with new endings, and speaking skills while presenting their completed work will be reviewed by the teacher.

Additional Resources

Related Websites

These two websites can provide students with more practice on making inferences about a text.

- Into the Book—http://reading.ecb.org/index.html
- BrainPOP Jr—www.brainpopjr.com/readingandwriting/comprehension/makeinferences/preview.weml.

Related Apps

- Inference Ace (free)—practice making inferences on an iPad.
- InferCabulary (free)—learn new vocabulary through making inferences on an iPad.

Further Reading

Hoyt, L. (2009). Revisit reflect retell: Time tested strategies for teaching reading comprehension. Portsmouth, NH: Heinemann.

TESOL PreK–12 English Language Proficiency Standards

Standard 1: English language learners communicate for social, intercultural, and instructional purposes within the school setting.

Standard 2: English language learners communicate information, ideas, and concepts necessary for academic success in the area of language arts.

Common Core State Standards ELA Suggested Connections

The following are the Common Core State Standards for English Language Arts that are aligned with this lesson. The rubric on the next page includes a sampling of grade levels to show how the standards get more complex at higher grade levels.

Writing: W.K.3; W.1.3; W.2.3; W.3.3; W.4.3; W.5.3; W.6.3; W.7.3; W.8.3; W.9–10.3; W.11–12.3

Speaking and Listening: SL.K.4; SL.1.4; SL.2.4; SL.3.4; SL.4.4; SL.5.4; SL.6.4; SL.7.4; SL.8.4; SL.9–10.4; SL.11–12.4

THE RED BOOK

CCSS Sample Rubric

Go to www.tesol.org/wordless to complete the rubric by adding your grade level standards from the Common Core website.

Writing: http://www.corestandards.org/ELA-Literacy/W/introduction/

Speaking and Listening: http://www.corestandards.org/ELA-Literacy/SL/introduction/

	Grading Criteria			
	Outstanding 10	Adequate 8–9	Developing 1–7	Not Present 0
	All of the criteria are present and fully developed.	Most of the criteria are present and adequately developed.	Some of the criteria are present and somewhat developed.	None of the criteria are present.
Standards	Teacher's Comments			
W.K.3. Use a combination of drawing, dictating, and writing to narrate a single event or several loosely linked events, tell about the events in the order in which they occurred, and provide a reaction to what happened.				
SL.K.4. Describe familiar people, places, things, and events and, with prompting and support, provide additional detail. *or*				
W.3.3. Write narratives to develop real or imagined experiences or events using effective technique, descriptive details, and clear event sequences.				

(continued)	Grading Criteria			
	Outstanding 10	**Adequate 8–9**	**Developing 1–7**	**Not Present 0**
	All of the criteria are present and fully developed.	Most of the criteria are present and adequately developed.	Some of the criteria are present and somewhat developed.	None of the criteria are present.
Standards	**Teacher's Comments**			
SL.3.4. Report on a topic or text, tell a story, or recount an experience with appropriate facts and relevant, descriptive details, speaking clearly at an understandable pace. *or*				
W.6.3. Write narratives to develop real or imagined experiences or events using effective technique, relevant descriptive details/ well-chosen details, and well-structured event sequences.				
SL.6.4. Present claims and findings, sequencing ideas logically and using pertinent descriptions, facts, and details to accentuate main ideas or themes; use appropriate eye contact, adequate volume, and clear pronunciation. *or*				

(continued)	Grading Criteria			
	Outstanding 10	**Adequate 8–9**	**Developing 1–7**	**Not Present 0**
	All of the criteria are present and fully developed.	Most of the criteria are present and adequately developed.	Some of the criteria are present and somewhat developed.	None of the criteria are present.
Standards	**Teacher's Comments**			
W.11–12.3. Write narratives to develop real or imagined experiences or events using effective technique, relevant descriptive details/ well-chosen details, and well-structured event sequences.				
SL.11–12.4. Present information, findings, and supporting evidence, conveying a clear and distinct perspective, such that listeners can follow the line of reasoning, alternative or opposing perspectives are addressed, and the organization, development, substance, and style are appropriate to purpose, audience, and a range of formal and informal tasks.				
Total points				

ZOOM

by Istvan Banyai

Lesson by Jessica S. Cohen and Gilda Martinez-Alba

Level	Beginning to advanced
Preparation Time	15 minutes
Length of Lesson	60 minutes
Objective	The students will create zoom picture stories with a clear beginning, middle, and end.

Materials

- *Zoom* by Istvan Banyaiby (New York, NY: Puffin Books, 1995)
- Color copies of several series of events zooming out from up close (e.g., a pink circle, an ice cream cone, a child eating the ice cream cone; a car, a car on a road, the car on the road on a TV, a person watching the TV), one picture for each student
- Paper, pencils, crayons

Vocabulary

- advertisement
- children
- city
- cruise
- earth
- farm
- island
- jet
- magazine

- Native American
- pilot
- rooster
- sleeping
- television
- village
- window
- zoom

Procedure

1. Do a picture walk. Go through the entire book, page by page, being sure to show each page long enough that the students can see what is happening in the beginning, middle, and end of the story. They need to understand that each page is zooming out from the previous page.

2. Pass out color copies of several series of events zooming out from up close, one picture for each student. (For example: A pink circle, an ice cream cone, a child eating the ice cream cone. A car, a car on a road, the car on the road on a TV, a person watching the TV.) Pass these out to the students and have them organize themselves by the pictures they have, in order from beginning to end.

3. Then, have students create their own "zoom" pictures, each group making their own set. The number of frames they create could be modified based on their level. Students at a beginning level could create a three-frame story, while more advanced students could create a six- or eight-frame story. You may choose to have students write a story to match their pictures, or you may choose to keep the wordless book form.

4. Last, have students read their stories to the class.

Assessment

The students' zoom picture stories will be reviewed by the teacher to determine if they have a clear beginning, middle, and end.

Additional Resources

Additional Books:

Students could read additional books by the same author:

Re-Zoom by Istvan Banyai (New York, NY: Puffin Books, 1998).

The Other Side by Istvan Banyai (San Francisco, CA: Chronicle Books, 2005).

Related Websites

Google Earth, which students could use to zoom in and out to look at different locations for follow-up—www.google.com/earth/.

Students could put together jigsaw puzzles at this website—www.jigzone.com/.

Related Apps

- What's the Pic? (free)— guess the picture by looking at a small part of the whole image.
- Sentence Builder (free)—build sentences, customized with your own pictures and sentences. Students can create sentences to go along with the pictures in the book *Zoom.*

Further Reading

Colorín Colorado. (2007). *Standards-based writing for ELLs.* Retrieved from http://www.colorincolorado.org/educators/teaching/writing/.

TESOL PreK–12 English Language Proficiency Standards

Standard 1: English language learners communicate for social, intercultural, and instructional purposes within the school setting.

Standard 2: English language learners communicate information, ideas, and concepts necessary for academic success in the area of language arts.

Common Core State Standards ELA Suggested Connections

The following are the Common Core State Standards for English Language Arts that are aligned with this lesson. The rubric on the next page includes a sampling of grade levels to show how the standards get more complex at higher grade levels.

Writing: W.K.3; W.1.3; W.2.3; W.3.3; W.4.3; W.5.3; W.6.3; W.7.3; W.8.3; W.9–10.3; W.11–12.3

ZOOM

CCSS Sample Rubrics

Go to www.tesol.org/wordless to complete the rubric by adding your grade level standards from the Common Core website.

Writing: http://www.corestandards.org/ELA-Literacy/W/introduction/

	Grading Criteria			
	Outstanding 10	**Adequate 8–9**	**Developing 1–7**	**Not Present 0**
	All of the criteria are present and fully developed.	Most of the criteria are present and adequately developed.	Some of the criteria are present and somewhat developed.	None of the criteria are present.
Standards	**Teacher's Comments**			
W.K.3. Use a combination of drawing, dictating, and writing to narrate a single event or several loosely linked events, tell about the events in the order in which they occurred, and provide a reaction to what happened. *or*				
W.3.3. Write narratives to develop real or imagined experiences or events using effective technique, descriptive details, and clear event sequences. *or*				
W.6.3–12.3. Write narratives to develop real or imagined experiences or events using effective technique, relevant descriptive details/ well-chosen details, and well-structured event sequences.				
Total points				

UNSPOKEN: A STORY FROM THE UNDERGROUND RAILROAD

by Henry Cole

Lesson by Matthew D. Vaughn-Smith

Level	Beginning to advanced
Preparation Time	5 minutes
Length of Lesson	50 minutes
Objective	Students will infer the events of the story using the pictures and their prior knowledge as evidence for their inferences and will design a comic strip of the story with captions based upon their inferences.

Materials

- *Unspoken: A Story from the Underground Railroad* by Henry Cole (New York, NY: Scholastic Press, 2012)
- Pencils and paper
- Laptop
- Comic creation software such as Comic Life (free trial available at www.comiclife.com)

Vocabulary

- barn
- bounty
- chickens
- chores
- cornfield

- curious
- farm
- lantern
- runaway
- slave
- slave master
- soldiers
- suspicious
- war

Procedure

1. Take a picture walk through the story, allowing students to reflect on the pictures in the beginning, middle, and end.
2. Assign students one or two scenes from the story. Give students a piece of paper to sketch out their ideas for a comic based on the scene.
3. Have students re-create the scenes using comic creation software such as Comic Life. The comic scene must have captions indicating the character's thoughts or what students think the characters would have said. More advanced ELs can visualize what is going on between each page then create a comic strip for their visualization.
4. Give each student a computer with the Comic Life software, and assist students in taking pictures for their comic.
5. Print out the scenes and have students place them in sequence. Have students share their class story.

Assessment

The students' comic strips will be reviewed by the teacher.

Additional Resources

Related Websites

An interactive experience in the Underground Railroad—http://education.nationalgeographic.com/education/media/underground-railroad-journey-freedom/?ar_a=1.

Information about the Underground Railroad and slavery in the United States—www.history.com/topics/black-history/underground-railroad.

Related Apps

- Strip Designer ($2.99)—create comic strips on an iPad or iPhone.
- Civil War: America's Epic Struggle ($4.99)—learn about the Civil War on an iPad or iPhone.

Further Reading

Schroeder, A. (2000). *Minty: A story of young Harriet Tubman.* New York, NY: Puffin.

TESOL PreK–12 English Language Proficiency Standards

Standard 1: English language learners communicate for social, intercultural, and instructional purposes within the school setting.

Standard 2: English language learners communicate information, ideas, and concepts necessary for academic success in the area of language arts.

Common Core State Standards ELA Suggested Connections

The following are the Common Core State Standards for English Language Arts that are aligned with this lesson. The rubric on the next page includes a sampling of grade levels to show how the standards get more complex at higher grade levels.

Writing: W.K.3; W.1.3; W.2.3; W.3.3; W.4.3; W.5.3; W.6.3; W.7.3; W.8.3; W.9–10.3; W.11–12.3

UNSPOKEN

CCSS Sample Rubric

Go to www.tesol.org/wordless to complete the rubric by adding your grade level standards from the Common Core website.

Writing: http://www.corestandards.org/ELA-Literacy/W/introduction/

	Grading Criteria			
	Outstanding 10	**Adequate 8–9**	**Developing 1–7**	**Not Present 0**
	All of the criteria are present and fully developed.	Most of the criteria are present and adequately developed.	Some of the criteria are present and somewhat developed.	None of the criteria are present.
Standards	**Teacher's Comments**			
W.K.3. Use a combination of drawing, dictating, and writing to narrate a single event or several loosely linked events, tell about the events in the order in which they occurred, and provide a reaction to what happened. *or*				
W.3.3. Write narratives to develop real or imagined experiences or events using effective technique, descriptive details, and clear event sequences. *or*				
W.6.3–12.3. Write narratives to develop real or imagined experiences or events using effective technique, relevant descriptive details/ well-chosen details, and well-structured event sequences.				
Total points				

REFERENCES AND IMAGE CREDITS

Baker, J. (2010). *Mirror.* Somerville, MA: Candlewick Press.

    MIRROR. Copyright © 2010 by Jeannie Baker. Reproduced by permission of the publisher, Candlewick Press, on behalf of Walker Books, London.

Banyai, I. (1995). *Zoom.* New York, NY: Puffin Books.

    Cover from ZOOM by Istvan Banyai. Copyright 1998. Used by permission of Penguin Random House. All rights reserved.

Becker, A. (2013). *Journey.* Somerville, MA: Candlewick Press.

    JOURNEY. Copyright © 2013 by Aaron Becker. Reproduced by permission of the publisher, Candlewick Press, Somerville, MA.

Briggs, R. (1978). *The snowman.* New York, NY: Random House Children's Books.

    Cover from THE SNOWMAN by Raymond Briggs. Copyright 1978. Used by permission of Penguin Random House LLC. All rights reserved.

Cole, H. (2012). *Unspoken: A story from the Underground Railroad.* New York, NY: Scholastic Press.

Day, A. (1996). *Good dog, Carl.* New York, NY: Little Simon.

Day, A. (2012). *Carl at the dog show.* New York, NY: Margaret Ferguson Books.

DePaola, T. (1978). *Pancakes for breakfast.* New York, NY: Harcourt.

    Cover from PANCAKES FOR BREAKFAST by Tomie DePaola. Cover illustration copyright © 1978 by Tomie dePaola. Reprinted by permission from Houghton Mifflin Publishing Company. All rights reserved.

Fleischman, P., & Hawkes, K. (2004). *Sidewalk circus.* Somerville, MA: Candlewick Press.

    SIDEWALK CIRCUS. Text copyright © 2004 by Paul Fleischman. Illustrations Copyright © 2004 by Kevin Hawkes. Reproduced by permission of the publisher, Candlewick Press, Somerville, MA.

Hoban, T. (1986). *Shapes, shapes, shapes.* New York, NY: Greenwillow Books.

Idle, M. (2013). *Flora and the flamingo.* San Francisco, CA: Chronicle Books.

    Cover from FLORA AND THE FLAMINGO by Molly Idle. Cover illustration copyright © 2013 by Molly Idle. Used with permission from Chronicle Books, San Francisco. Please visit www.ChonicleBooks.com.

Lee, S. (2008). *Wave.* San Francisco, CA: Chronicle Books.

Cover from WAVE by Suzy Lee. Cover illustration copyright © 2008 by Suzy Lee. Used with permission from Chronicle Books, San Francisco. Please visit www.ChonicleBooks.com.

Lehman, B. (2004). *The red book.* Boston, MA: Houghton Mifflin.

Cover from THE RED BOOK by Barbara Lehman. Jacket art copyright © 2004 by Barbara Lehman. Reprinted by permission of Houghton Mifflin Harcourt Publishing Company. All rights reserved.

Lehman, B. (2007). *Rainstorm.* Boston, MA: Houghton Mifflin.

Cover from RAINSTORM by Barbara Lehman. Jacket art copyright © 2007 by Barbara Lehman. Reprinted by permission from Houghton Mifflin Publishing Company. All rights reserved.

Mayer, M. (1967). *A boy, a dog, and a frog.* New York, NY: Dial Books for Young Readers.

Pinkney, J. (2009). *The lion and the mouse.* New York, NY: Little, Brown and Company.

Rodriguez, B. (2009). *The chicken thief.* Brooklyn, NY: Enchanted Lion Books.

Cover from THE CHICKEN THIEF by Barbara Rodriguez. Jacket art used with permission from Enchanted Lion Books.

Rohmann, E. (2002). *My friend rabbit.* New York, NY: Square Fish.

Thomson, B. (2010). *Chalk.* New York, NY: Amazon Children's Publishing.

Wiesner, D. (1988). *Free fall.* New York, NY: Harper Collins.

Wiesner, D. (1991). *Flotsam.* New York, NY: Clarion Books.

Cover from FLOTSAM by David Wiesner. Jacket illustrations copyright © 2006 by David Wiesner. Reprinted by permission of Clarion Books, an imprint of Houghton Mifflin Harcourt Publishing Company. All rights reserved.

Wiesner, D. (1991). *Tuesday.* New York, NY: Clarion Books.

Cover from TUESDAY by David Wiesner. Jacket illustrations copyright © 1991 by David Wiesner. Reprinted by permission of Clarion Books, an imprint of Houghton Mifflin Harcourt Publishing Company. All rights reserved.

Wiesner, D. (2013). *Mr. Wuffles!* New York, NY: Clarion Books.

Cover from MR. WUFFLES! by David Wiesner. Jacket illustrations copyright © 2003 by David Wiesner. Reprinted by permission of Clarion Books, an imprint of Houghton Mifflin Harcourt Publishing Company. All rights reserved.